More Advanced Praise for *Aquarius Now*

"'The inner revolution is the heart of world revolution,' Marilyn Ferguson writes, perceptively, in this important book. Much as the Great Awakening presaged the American Revolution, future historians may identify the Consciousness Revolution . . . as having laid the foundation for whatever great events may occur over the next few decades."
—William Strauss and Neil Howe, coauthors
of *Generations* and *The Fourth Turning*

"Marilyn Ferguson has returned just when we need her the most to inject us with her fierce optimism about the responsibility and potentiality that each of us has to make the world a better place. Readers will appreciate the great generosity of spirit she displays in her call to action. The 16th century gave birth to *wunderkammern* or curiosity cabinets in which individuals collected wondrous and strange bits of nature and art to celebrate the marvels of the universe. Marilyn Ferguson fashions *Aquarius Now* as a wunderkammern of information to celebrate the universal connections of the human spirit."
—John Briggs, author of *Trickster Tales, Fractals: The Patterns of Chaos*, and *Fire in the Crucible*; coauthor of *Seven Life Lessons of Chaos* and *Turbulent Mirror*

"Ferguson, to whom we owe so much, again gives us a brilliant, intense, fast-paced and engrossing work as valuable to us today as her offering twenty-five years ago. The clouds of despair have grown darker, and Marilyn's astonishing vitality, acute awareness, and buoyant optimism are needed now more than ever. May her number increase and her books flourish."
—Joseph Chilton Pearce, author of *Magical Child* and *Spiritual Initiation and the Breakthrough of Consciousness*

"We have entered the Knight Time—a moment in history in which we, like warriors of former times, must summon the courage and skills to confront the challenges we face as a people and as a planet. For those seeking inspiration, you're holding it in your hands. Marilyn Ferguson's *Aquarius Now* is a blueprint for a future that begins with you. Read and heed, America, while there is still time."
—Larry Dossey, M.D., author of *The Extraordinary Healing Power of Ordinary Things, Reinventing Medicine*, and *Healing Words*

"For many decades, Marilyn Ferguson has had the uncanny ability to predict cultural trends and to fathom their implications for the future of our world. *Aquarius Now* is a remarkable book, one that not only portrays a road map for society but also shows each of us how we can collaborate with our fellow human beings to re-draw that map to evoke a planet where play supplants war and where ecological awareness replaces environmental destruction."

—Stanley Krippner, coauthor of *The Psychological Impact of War Trauma on Civilians* and co-editor of *Extraordinary Dreams and How to Work With Them*

"Marilyn Ferguson's *Aquarius Now* is indeed a welcome reminder as we make our way through the new millennium. She not only writes well with passion, new information, and a great grasp of history, she also lets us know now what this new age we are living through is really all about. If you haven't got a clue, then read this book, tune in, join the age, and enjoy it. If you have a clue, then open your eyes for she has some new insights to share."

—Fred Alan Wolf, Ph.D., National Book Award winning author of many books, audio CDs, and featured star in the movie *What the Bleep Do We Know?!*

"Like Tom Paine, Marilyn Ferguson calls for a common sense that is radical for our time yet urgently needed for our evolution. Let us hope that we take this leap."

—Connie Zweig, Ph.D., author of *The Holy Longing* and *The Moth to the Flame: The Life Story of Rumi*

"Marilyn Ferguson, whose groundbreaking work with Brain/Mind Bulletin helped launch a whole new way of looking at the world, always keeps us honest and keeps us thinking. *Aquarius Now* draws from a multitude of sources to inspire readers to give up fear-based living and reclaim our native common sense. *Aquarius Now* paves the way to a future we want to live in. Take its message to heart."

—Ken Dychtwald, Ph.D., author of *Bodymind*, *The Age Wave*, and *The Power Years*

"*Aquarius Now* begins a conversation—inner reflection and dialogue with others—that any reader will be eager to join. It is a timely and outrageous achievement."

—Richard Lang, Chairman and Co-founder, *Burst.com*

AQUARIUS NOW

Radical Common Sense and Reclaiming Our Personal Sovereignty

Marilyn Ferguson

Boston, MA/York Beach, ME

First published in 2005 by
RED WHEEL/WEISER, LLC
York Beach, ME
With offices at:
368 Congress Street
Boston, MA 02210
www.redwheelweiser.com

Library of Congress Cataloging-in-Publication Data

Ferguson, Marilyn.
Aquarius now : radical common sense and reclaiming our personal
sovereignty / Marilyn Ferguson.
p. cm.
ISBN 1-57863-369-9
1. Radicalism. 2. Conduct of life. 3. Social action.
4. New Age movement. I. Title.

HN65.F46 2005
303.48'4--dc22   2005014294

Typeset in 11 point Stone Serif by Sky Peck Design

Printed in Canada
FR

12 11 10 09 08 07 06 05

8 7 6 5 4 3 2 1

The paper used in this publication meets the minimum requirements of the
American National Standard for Information Sciences—Permanence of Paper
for Printed Library Materials Z39.48-1992 (R1997).

I believe in aristocracy . . . Not an aristocracy of power, based upon rank and influence, but an aristocracy of the sensitive, the considerate, and the plucky. Its members are to be found in all nations and classes and all through the ages, and there is a secret understanding between them when they meet. They represent the true human tradition, the one permanent victory of our queer race over cruelty and chaos. Thousands of them perish in obscurity, a few are great names. They are sensitive for others as well as themselves, they are considerate without being fussy, their pluck is not swankiness but the power to endure, and they can take a joke.

—E. M. FORSTER

For Emily, Evan, Juli, and Katherine

CONTENTS

ACKNOWLEDGMENTS

THANKS TO MY PUBLISHER, Red Wheel/Weiser, for their enthusiasm and commitment . . . to Jan Johnson, publisher, for the level of engagement she demanded, for the times she conceded, and the times she stuck to her guns. Thanks to Brenda Knight for her insights, to Michael Kerber, Rachel Leach, Kate Hartke, Bonni Hamilton, Mike Conlon, and Gary Hill. Paul Caubet, business manager for *Brain/Mind* and a visionary artist, proposed the term "radical common sense" for the sudden insights and unexpected answers that emerge from a state of heightened attention.

Eric Ferguson, who cut short his extended stay in London to take on editorial responsibilities for *Brain/Mind Bulletin*, whose support and patience have been unflagging, and thanks, too, to Susanne, his Danish-born wife.

Thanks to Jason Keehne, Greg Wright, Sylvia Delgado, Eric Gould, Viola Owen, Kris Ferguson, Lynn Ferguson, Anita Storey, Perry Carrison, and other alumni of *Brain/Mind*; William Shanley; Phil Harrington, Kim and Wayne Bechtold, Ray and Kindred Gottlieb, Jytte Lokvig, Charlie Myers, Paula Litsky, Richard Lang, Lisa Walters, Mel Werbach, Bill Domke, Anne Rodgers, Lynnea Bylund, Todd Dougherty, Jim Channon, Fred Lehrman, Stuart Heller, Sandra Seagal, Ruth Strassburg, Armand DiMele, Rinaldo and Shanna Brutoco, Ingo Swann, Jean Houston, Russell Singer, Tom ____, Gale and Roy Gordon, Jerome Josph, and Patricia Morrison.

To paraphrase Winston Churchill, "Never has one person owed so much to so many." So many colleagues and even strangers have contributed immeasurably to this and kindred projects over the years that in no way is this a complete accounting. Those I forgot to acknowledge who I overlooked you know who you are. Please forgive the oversight and know that you are thanked.

INTRODUCTION

The student asked, "How long must one remain in the dark?"
I said, "Until one can see in the dark."

—FLORENCE SCOVEL SHINN

The Aquarian Conspiracy, first published in 1980, described a positive movement, international and informally organized, whose members were deeply affected by transformative events and who wanted to create a more humane society based on what they were discovering.

In writing that book, I had greatly underestimated the legions of people who were scanning the radar for news about this nameless movement and looking for new friends to help ease the loneliness of their journey.

Little did we realize how soon millions of people all over the world would be talking about nothing else. But in those early days the conspirators worked their quiet revolutions—emphasizing creativity in a job training program, teaching university courses on mysticism and brain hemisphere specialization, finding the cutting-edge science news to put in Sunday sermons.

Over time a new industry arose, offering a staggering variety of health products, musical instruments from India, audio tapes and an explosion of books on alternative healing, self-help, Jungian psychology, twelve-step programs, angels from every angle, and innumerable classes, seminars, conferences, television shows, CD-ROMs, and documentaries.

Well-known figures in the movement were featured in *People* magazine. Popular gurus and stand up comics with a transpersonal rap were playing at Hollywood clubs.

The dissemination of a larger scientific and social worldview meant something personally to thousands of people who had long suspected that there was something shaky about the old one.

In the meantime, some innovative seminar leaders and I created an unusual seminar—seven presenters and forty participants. Not a very cost-effective ratio, but the series of seminars had been designed as an experiment for gathering information for the book you are reading.

Aquarius Now: Radical Common Sense and Reclaiming Our Personal Sovereignty is about how to thrive in a time of escalating change. It is an attempt to reclaim the word "radical" from its current usage meaning "extremist." It's about the visionary in everyone and how we can break out of our prisons. It's about how our brains can work for us or against us, and how we can wake up in the dark.

There are those who oppose the idea of radically upgrading the collective intelligence. They fear that if they don't reject such proposals they will eventually become extinct.

It is a dark, unspoken truth that the powerful—the "ruling class"—make up the rules as they go along. Public policy is designed by spin doctors who aim to keep our heads below the water. The public good is not a consideration and, their self-serving agendas prevail over common sense.

They have prevailed too long, often by appealing to that part of us that wants more for less. We're afraid to play the game for fear we'll suffer more discomfort than we do in our present condition.

Therein lies our shame.

What we need now is not another formula or doctrine but

a set of operating procedures. We have to become a tribe of strategists on the move, ingenious toolmakers, visionary designers. There are no experienced guides to take us safely on the journey. Just our own awakened selves.

Most of us are suspicious of hidden agendas including, if we're honest about it, our own. Who, or what, is at fault? We like to blame our woes on institutions, political parties, government agencies, schools, big business, labor, capitalism, socialism. Or we blame the entire system.

But let us acknowledge, here and now, that social policy is always determined by individuals. Cultural breakthroughs have always resulted from the insights and effort of individuals. New behaviors are initially modeled by individuals.

The ferment and viability in any society is directly proportionate to the number of people actively living their ideas. This is not positive thinking—it is positive action: the spirit of experiment.

In this spirit, people learn from each other—old and young, priests and healers, merchants and artists, warriors and peacemakers, politicians and scribes. They cheer each other on, and everyone wins because society wins. In this larger game, no one takes pleasure in the defeat of another. Victory doesn't lie in taming our nature but in progressively discovering and revealing more of it. We evolve into a moving species of change and renewal. We consistently challenge our many selves. We are deeply intuitive in all our affairs and incredibly in tune with the energies of the people and nature around us.

We explore as we move. We heal and nourish our bodies and souls out of splendid habit. We lead our world through enlightened measures of service. We accomplish our tasks with precision and genius. We are a great and mighty people, the new nomads, and our travels have led us to that Utopian place from the ancient future. The place of running waters, whispering winds, and moving foundations. From that tribe of free saints in perpetual motion, we call the selves we were meant to be.

Becoming a new kind of people . . . that's an outrageous goal. On the other hand, dare we ignore the one option that might ensure a new social contract? Conventional wisdom says it can't be done. Radical common sense says we're foolish not to try.

1

WE HAVE IT
IN OUR POWER

A New Method of Thinking

The time hath found us.

—THOMAS PAINE, *COMMON SENSE*

On January 10, 1776, a recent English immigrant published a pamphlet urging American colonists to rethink their assumptions about something most people took for granted: the divine right of monarchy. According to contemporary reports, many affirmed Royalists were converted by a single reading of Thomas Paine's *Common Sense*. Paine must indeed have argued well; half a million copies were sold over the next year, an astonishing number given a total population in the colonies of just over two million.

Because Paine assigned the royalties from his two-shilling pamphlet to the revolutionary cause, after the war a grateful United States Congress awarded him a small pension and a farm in upstate New York. Yet only a few years later, Paine was branded a traitor for expanding further on the meaning of democracy. At one moment he was a hero, the father of reason; shortly thereafter, an outcast.

What is this thing called common sense? We appeal to it incessantly, but it eludes definition. The very term implies a body of information that everyone knows, yet we ruefully agree that nothing is rarer than common sense. The French do not have an exact equivalent of the English phrase *common sense*. Rather they say *le bon sens,* the good sense, and they do not take it for granted.

Although we speak of common sense as if it were static and agreed-upon, in fact it evolves. In the eighteenth and nineteenth centuries, for example, Europeans considered bathing unhealthy. It was widely believed that tomatoes were poisonous until the eighteenth century when a man ate one on the courthouse steps in Salem, New Jersey, as a demonstration.

As the evidence becomes unassailable, a new common sense emerges.

Common sense is sometimes subjective. What one person considers sensible strikes another as wrong-headed. Common sense is also shaped by cultural and even sub-cultural values. One group's foregone conclusions are another's heresy.

Common sense is rooted in local assumptions. We deem a belief common sense when we no longer recall its origins. Some common sense is felt in agreement, values that seem so self-evident they aren't even discussed unless violated, as when people are blatantly acting against their own interests.

More and more often we are asking each other, "What ever happened to common sense?" A rhetorical question, maybe, but it bears examining. With the benefit of hindsight, we can see the inadequacy of the notion of common sense as a body of information. Even so, we seem to agree that something is missing. We may not be able to explain it, but we know it when we see it.

When we say that someone has common sense we usually mean a kind of practical balance. Such a person is in control without being rigid and is capable of spontaneous behavior without taking foolish risks.

It could be said that common sense is a way of being in the world, a function or an attitude rather than a body of knowledge—not thoughts but the ability to think freshly and purposefully. Common sense is not what we know but how we know it.

Common sense is remembering what we have learned and remembering that we forget. It takes its own ignorance, biases, and errors into account. It wants to learn even when the lessons are hard. It is a subtle sense of consequences and possibilities.

Our Runaway Societies

The final scenes of Emile Zola's *The Beast in Man* demonstrate a failure of classical common sense. An irate engineer and fireman are quarreling in the locomotive of a passenger train. In his rage the fireman has stoked the engine's fire into an inferno. The two begin struggling. They clutch each other by the throat, each trying to force the other through the open door. Losing their balance, both tumble out and roll down the steep mountainside. The train hurtles onward, picking up speed. The hapless passengers, soldiers en route to the front, are dozing or drunkenly partying, unaware of the impending disaster.

Zola's story is a parable of modern societies and their runaway institutions. Those supposedly in charge, embroiled in their own personal dramas, paralyzed with performance anxiety or preoccupied with their ambitions, have left their driver's seats. Meanwhile, we, their oblivious passengers, are about to pay the price. Unless, of course, we wake up.

One looks as hard and cynically for an honest culture as Diogenes searched for an honest man. In many countries, merchants and manufacturers are spending ever more to attract an ever more skeptical public. Television viewers and newspaper readers mistrust much of what they hear and see. Respect for institutions, even for religion, is in decline.

Few of our designated leaders offer credible comfort. High confusion translates into chaotic policy. People everywhere seem to be acknowledging the gap between the ideal and the reality, and we can't figure out who is at fault. Scapegoats—the infamous "they" and "them"—are in short supply.

In the Zen tradition there is the tale of a young farmer who owned a treasured heirloom, a large and decorative glass bottle. One day a young gosling wandered into the farmhouse, fell into the bottle, and could not be extricated. Because the tender-hearted farmer could not bring himself to harm a living creature, he could not kill the goose. But neither could he bring himself to destroy the precious bottle. Out of kindness and indecision he kept feeding the gosling. Every day the crisis seemed more imminent.

The *koan,* or Zen riddle: *How will the farmer remove the goose from the bottle?*

Surely this is our story, humanity in the Twentieth Century, polluting and populating and quarreling, tearing a hole in the very fabric of our atmosphere. Living systems throttled more and more each day by our time-hallowed structures and the limits of our resources. Us in the bottle.

Radical Common Sense

When we got organized as a country and we wrote a fairly radical constitution with a radical amount of individual freedom to Americans, it was assumed that the Americans who had that freedom would use it responsibly.

—BILL CLINTON

To get out of the bottle we need *radical* common sense. Radical common sense is common sense deliberately encouraged and applied. Radical common sense reflects the growing realization that individual good sense in not enough—that society itself must make sense or decline. Radical common sense is a spirit. It respects the past, it pays attention to the present, and therefore it can imagine a more workable future.

On the one hand, it looks as if modern civilization hasn't the time, resources, or determination to make it through the neck of the bottle. We can't get there from here. We can't solve our deepest problems through such traditional strategies as competition, wishful thinking, struggle, or war. We can't frighten people (including ourselves) into being good or smart or healthy. We find we can't educate by rote or by bribery, we can't win by cheating, we can't buy peace at the expense of others, and, above all, we can't fool Mother Nature.

On the other hand, maybe the answers lie in the problem—our thinking, especially our ideas that nature is to be mastered rather than understood. We have tried to run roughshod over certain powerful realities.

Radical common sense says let's ally ourselves with nature. We have nothing to lose and a great deal to gain. As the old saying has it, "if you can't beat 'em, join 'em." We can apprentice at nature's side, working with her secrets respectfully rather than trying to steal them. For example, scientists who observe natural systems report that nature is more cooperative ("Live and let live") than competitive ("Kill or be killed"). "Competing" species, it turns out, often co-exist by food- and time-sharing; they feed at different hours on different parts of the same plant. Among moose and some other herd animals, the old or injured members offer themselves to predators, allowing younger and healthier members to escape.

Altruism appears to serve an evolutionary function in living creatures. In its inventiveness, nature—including human nature—may be on our side.

By documenting the health benefits of such traditional virtues as persistence, hard work, forgiveness, and generosity, scientific research is validating both common sense and idealism. People who have discovered a purpose feel better, like themselves more, age more subtly, and live longer.

Radical common sense derives its conviction from science *and* from the inspired examples of individuals.

The Lessons of "Living Treasures"

Japanese society has an admirable habit of honoring its outstanding contributors as if they were national resources. Individuals who have developed their abilities to a high level or who have given generously of themselves are designated "living treasures."

Every nation, indeed every neighborhood, has its living treasures, people who find their greatest reward in contributing to the society. Some are well known, but millions are quietly going about their heroic tasks perfecting their work, trying to serve more, not less.

Most of these people grasp the content of the body of wisdom Aldous Huxley called the Perennial Philosophy. They recognize that their fate is tied to that of others. They know that they must take responsibility, maintain their integrity, keep learning, and dream boldly. And they know that this knowing is not enough.

They are making clear that what they need now is the so-called "nitty gritty," the small steps that precede a leap. They want a technology transfer from the people who make their dreams come true.

Radical common sense says that we should collect and disseminate such secrets for the good of the whole. And, not surprisingly, that most capable people are not only happy to share what they have learned; they are also eager to benefit from the experience of others.

It is little wonder that our individual discoveries don't become common knowledge. When we stumble across certain tricks and short-cuts we usually don't think to tell anyone else. For one thing, they probably already know. Or we're competitive.

The more successful we become at our chosen tasks, the less time there is for analysis and reflection. The coach may recall that the gold-medal figure skater was once graceless or fearful. Certain psychological and technical breakthroughs made the difference. The champion, also a subtle observer of change, is too busy mastering new moves to spell out the anatomy of a winning performance. The same could be said of the outstanding entrepreneur, statesman, or parent. They aren't teaching because they are so busy learning.

Think for a moment of your own breakthroughs. Did you record and track your learning? Most of the time we notice improvement in retrospect, if at all. And we rarely think to mark the trail for others to follow. "Live and learn," we say, acknowledging the value of experience. We usually forget about "Live and teach."

Radical common sense says that our collective survival may depend on our ability to teach ourselves and others. By pooling and organizing the wisdom of many scouts we can assemble a kind of guide and companion for travelers everywhere.

Apply certain laws of life, and you have nature on the side of your dream. You are less reliant on luck and, at the same time, better equipped to take advantage of it. You can contribute your best without compromising your values, undermining your health, or exploiting others. You can be an explorer and friend to humanity.

Achievers have an enabling attitude, realism, and a conviction that they themselves were the laboratory of innovation. Their ability to change themselves is central to their success. They have learned to conserve their energy by minimizing the time spent in regret or complaint. Every event is a lesson to them, every person a teacher. Learning is their true occupation, and out of it flowed their profession.

These four-minute-milers of the spirit insist that they are not unusually endowed, that others can do what they have done. They know factors of success more reliable than luck or native ability.

The not-so-hidden agenda is the conviction that leadership must become a grassroots phenomenon if our societies are to thrive. If that strikes you as unlikely, consider first of all that nothing else is likely to work. And secondly, be aware that people already secretly suspect that they are capable of taking charge. Sociological surveys have shown repeatedly that most people believe themselves smarter, more caring, more honest, and more responsible than most people.

Apparently we can't show these traits because "it's a jungle out there." It's as if to be "smart" we must hide our caring lest we try to live up to our responsibility in the jungle. So the dangerous jungle persists as a self-fulfilling prophecy from our collective self-image. One of the ways we can spring the goose from the bottle is to unite as free and honorable individuals who have the nerve and good sense to challenge defeatist assumptions. In so doing we have to pierce the veil that separates our heroes from the heroic in ourselves.

As our societies go through their identity crises, we can view the chaos as a sign of life, the turbulence as a healing fever. Radical common sense paraphrases Socrates: The unexamined *collective* life is not worth living.

The more sensitive I am as an individual, the more permeable I am to healthy new influences, the likelier that I can be molded into an unprecedented Self. That Self is the secret of success of a society. It sees the ways in which its fate is joined to the whole. It has the attributes we sometimes call soul and the passion we have called patriotism.

Radical common sense is the wisdom gleaned from the past that recognizes the perishable opportunities of the moment. It is the willingness to admit error and the refusal to be deterred by failure. Heroism, it becomes apparent, is nothing more than becoming our latent selves. Victory doesn't lie in transcending or taming our nature but in progressively discovering and revealing more of it.

Great problems, like the wars of old, may be a stimulus to achievement, but we don't have to rely on external challenge. Radical common sense says we can challenge ourselves. Or as the Taoist tradition puts it, we can embrace the tiger.

When asked for his most important discovery, a famous corporate trainer said, "I finally realized that people learn from only one thing: experience. And most people aren't very good at it."

Beyond a certain point all education is self-education. New

learning comes slowly unless we choose it. A self-defined challenge is an irresistible teacher.

In encompassing the simple secrets of the visionary life,
radical common sense may be the long-sought Grail, a powerful vessel in which we might shape ourselves and be shaped.

The Forerunner Self

"I don't want to be a butterfly," the caterpillar said,
"because I've never been one."

—STEWART EDWARD WHITE

At any time we are capable of stumbling into valuable new
behavior. We might call this phenomenon the Forerunner Self.
We grope, blunder, or wander our way into new avenues. If
we're alert to such changes or if they are pointed out by others, they will consolidate more quickly.

Radical common sense tells us that as we catch glimpses of
a more integrated, "higher" self, our task is to unify the knowledge fragmented by old traumas. Maybe inside each of us
there's a wise self trying to take charge.

The death inherent in transformation is like the snake's
sloughing of a skin or the pupa shedding its cocoon. The death
is just letting go of trying to stay the same. It is the radical shift
of birth.

Humanity's greatest presumption is our effort to stop the
river, to arrest inevitable change. To invoke the metaphor of
Zola's train, we have been fretting over our individual timeta-
bles and cabin comforts when the train itself is hurtling ahead
without our conscious guidance.

Our venerable institutions, the repositories of our beliefs
and values, need retooling if they are to regain our trust and
pride. A Forerunner Society may need to establish innovation
and truth as traditions rather than desperate last measures.

Virgil, the Latin poet, wrote *Novo ordus seclorum,* "A new age begins," a motto inscribed on United States dollar bills. The dream of a new beginning is recurrent, yet there are historical periods when deep cultural change seems more imminent.

Those who see the present era as a New Age are right on at least one count: Unprecedented numbers of people are pursuing visionary arts once restricted to the leisure classes and religious elites. Much of so-called New Age thinking is a kind of realistic idealism, the art and science of leading a rewarding life.

"We have it in our power to begin the world again," Thomas Paine told his compatriots. It was a young and presumptuous dream, but in a way the dreamers were right. We should not become so ashamed of the disappointments and travesties of democracy that we become ashamed of the idea itself. It is the outer reflection of our self-acceptance.

And we can begin in our individual lives to initiate more democracy among our parts; we can help reconcile the apparent differences of our own competing inner agendas. We can free our thoughts, tame our emotions, and strengthen our bodies to be clearer and more productive.

In the literal sense of the phrase, we can take charge.

We can capture the energy we have expanded in negative emotion and turn it to a useful task. We can find an inner Niagara that will power our ideas and put them to work. We don't have to give up any part of ourselves, not the skeptic nor the visionary, to live up to our own ideals.

And if enough of us take charge of our own lives, demanding our rights and the rights of others, paying more than our fair share and multiplying our rewards through stewardship, we indeed have it in our power to begin the world again.

And we begin by seeing with new eyes.

A TIME TO MOVE

The New Visionaries Are Revolutionaries
with Radical Common Sense

Common sense is genius in its working clothes.

—RALPH WALDO EMERSON

I don't give a damn about semi-radicals. . . .
This is not a time of gentleness.
It is not a time of lukewarm beginnings.
It is a time for open speech and fearless thinking.

—HELEN KELLER

From the earliest times until quite recently, troubled societies had a straightforward, if not simple, solution: Move. Find a new home. An entire tribe or nation would pick up its tents and treasures and relocate.

Migration has been at the heart of the human story since our ancestors left their Mesopotamian garden. Tribes have crossed the Siberian steppes, dispersed throughout the Middle East, sailed off to populate remote islands. In our own time, great numbers of Tibetans moved to India, Jews to Israel, and Vietnamese boat people to whatever port would have them.

Migrations are typically motivated by a dwindling of resources, political or religious persecution, or warlike neighbors. Then again, sometimes a people moves en masse because scouts and travelers carry tales of a distant land that is fruitful and temperate.

Modern civilization is in fact a Great Tribe that must now move or perish. Plagues and pestilences, droughts and wars, and pollution and diminishing resources have made it impossible for us to remain where we are. We must leave this familiar world of habitual strife and irrational priorities.

The only sensible course is to seek a new habitat.

In every nation, every tribe, every village, in our churches and temples and town squares, and in the dreams of our artists, we've heard of a better place. Let's call this place the Rumored Land. In such a place the waters would be clean and the natives would be kind. And where would such a place be found in this "small world"? Where on earth can we go?

The place we are moving toward, of course, is a new understanding.

A Successful Migration

A successful migration depends on the ingenuity of the tools we create along the way.

- Vision: A credible picture of what we might do and where we might go.

- Values: The return to classic values like kindness, willingness to work, and civic responsibility, and newer values like caring for the environment.

- Purpose: Meaningful causes or projects that can unite groups of people.

- Common sense: A demonstrated awareness of facts and consequences.

- Action: It's all within our ability. Somebody *do* something.

We are concerned about an apparent shortage of solutions and ideas, a lack of caring and meaning, a lack of understanding, and the failure of will. These perceived lacks, with their power to demoralize us, may be more immediately threatening to human survival than the predicted shortages of water, fuel, and even oxygen.

Without our wits and wills, we won't be able to strategize our way through the imminent crises in the physical realm. These observations help to determine our values. We are motivated to work toward ends that strike us as both right and reasonable.

Our values then move us. They direct us to act—but values alone do not always clarify which acts will accomplish our aims. Should our society punish lawbreakers more harshly? Should we emphasize moral education? Or should we determine whether or not the laws are just?

The word *value* derives from the Latin root *val*, referring to courage of character. What do you care about and for what are you willing to risk yourself? Values cannot be held passively. By definition, what you value is what you would do battle for. That's why hand-me-down values ("Honesty is the best policy") are not especially motivating until we have stumbled upon their truth for ourselves. Identifying the hierarchy of our values can help clarify the form our action should take.

Our authentic values also tend to shape an overarching purpose. And a sense of meaning demands we envision a solution, a fresh scenario.

A Lesson from the Renaissance

The convergence of events that catalyzed the Renaissance in Italy has its parallels in our time. Gutenberg's invention of the printing press made it possible for people to read about scientific discoveries. These reports—the "news"—shifted the public dialogue. The medieval preoccupation with angels faded as human beings discovered the marvels of nature and their own potential. The explosion of science, invention, sculpture, painting, architecture, and philosophy inspired the citizens of Florence to envision a new world, "without war and without humbug."

Exploding digital technology, the Internet, especially the World Wide Web, may be harbingers of a global renaissance. Millions of bloggers, linked and having their say, call to mind Jefferson's remark that if he had to choose between government without newspapers or newspapers without government, he would choose newspapers.

Global patterns of migration and diaspora in the twenty-first century dwarf the influx into Florence of Greek philosophers banished from Constantinople.

In a period we might call a "renaissance window," people from a variety of disciplines and social strata see that they can pull together for a common cause. They—we—share a common sense that technology and imagination can be married in some new way. State-of-the-art communications stimulate talk of participatory democracy. Citizens could express their views—"the common sense" of a situation.

At this point we should ask ourselves where do renaissances go? Why do they flourish and fade?

Florence is still a breathtaking flower among cities. How did she lose the impetus of the Renaissance, what happened to the new world "without war and without humbug"?

The great families that ruled Florence were bankers. Many, the Medicis especially, patrons of Leonardo, Michelangelo, Botticelli, and Della Robbia, were generous and civic-minded. They were agile when it came to avoiding war, but their riches came from financing other people's wars.

The coffers that built a church or cathedral on every corner and supported an army of artists and artisans were continually replenished by "blood money."

In that sense the citizens of Florence betrayed their own ideals, and one fine day Florence fell to invaders who coveted her wealth. Is this a morality tale for industrialized countries that encourage weapons manufacturers and financiers to sell their products to combatants in other countries, often to both sides?

"He who lives by the bottom line shall die by the bottom line. . . ."?

Last Call for Vision

Vision is directed imagination. It's not the goal but a goal-setting mechanism, a capacity to avert disasters and imagine preferred destinations. We may idly imagine having a flat tire, dying, going broke, getting rich. Directed imagination conceives outcomes clearly and takes them seriously enough to inspire real effort.

What our societies need now is not only leaders with vision, but support and training for vision itself. This has its parallel in the familiar saying: "Give a man a fish, and you feed him for a day; teach him to fish, and you feed him for a lifetime."

Visionary leaders might get us through dark nights, but we need to know how to light our own fires. An age of discovery is at hand, according to James Burke, creator of the BBC television series, *Connections*. Soon everyone will be expected to think like an innovator. The accelerating rate of change will call upon "ordinary citizens . . . to make leaps of the imagination that were traditionally expected of none but the most creative."

Biochemist Robert Root-Bernstein told a gathering of American scientists that "the cultural split will be between those who innovate and create and those who do not."

Thomas Paine's *Common Sense* called upon the American colonists to declare their independence. "Now is the seed time," he proclaimed. "A new era for politics is struck . . . a new method of thinking has arisen."

In white-hot language Paine laid out his argument against the divine right of kings, claiming to offer "nothing more than simple facts, plain arguments, and common sense." It was the right of people to choose—even to become—their own leaders. "We have it in our power to begin the world again," Paine wrote, and the age of popular revolutions was launched.

Today a deeply entrenched force still awaits overthrow by "a new method of thinking." This time the enemy is not so much a tyrant but rather the passivity that empowers all tyrants; not a historical king, but our perennial reluctance to assume the sovereignty of ourselves.

This time we haven't a need for assemblies to write declarations or wage wars. The fruits of this revolution will be increasingly evident as ever greater numbers of people take charge of their lives and responsibility for the world. Their decision is quickened by the simple, ironic recognition that every avenue of rescue appears to be blocked but one: the radical common sense to do the right thing, fueled by our ideals, the promptings of our better moments, our "high-mindedness."

The old idealism is the new common sense.

The Unfinished Revolution

The founders drew many ideas from various cultures: ancient Greece, France, England, and other European nations, and Native Americans.

The original framers expected the Constitution to evolve over the years. Thomas Jefferson himself maintained that every generation deserved its own revolution: "Can one generation bind another and all others in succession forever? I think not. The Creator made the earth for the living, not the dead."

Benjamin Rush, the patriot who encouraged Paine to write *Common Sense*, warned that too many people were mistaking the American War for the American Revolution. "The War is ended," he said, "but the first act of the Revolution has just begun."

Samuel Adams, grieving over the postwar excesses he saw in his beloved Boston, asked the question that haunts us still: "Alas, will men never be free?"

As Edward Gibbon wrote of another historic experiment in democracy:

> In the end, more than they wanted freedom, they wanted security. When the Athenians finally wanted not to give to society but for society to give to them,

when the freedom they wished for was freedom from responsibility, then Athens ceased to be free.

Enduring freedom is never free. It goes hand in hand with certain creative responsibilities: to take charge of ourselves, to pursue our best ideas, and to obey the imperatives of conscience.

Even our so-called right to the freedom of the press is hindered by powerful political interests that control the media, corrupt the truth, and cover up scandals. In this pivotal time we can go the way of the ancient Athenians or we can choose to take hold of liberty.

Liberty must be claimed and reclaimed amid the turbulence of daily life: pressures of time, pressures to conform, advertising propaganda, economic and other environmental stressors.

Liberty is what we make of our freedom.

Radical Common Sense

Common sense originally meant the consensus of all of one's senses. In the 1543 *Oxford English Dictionary* we find: "The eyes were ordained by nature that they might carry visible things to the common sense."

In 1606: "Common sense is a power or faculty of the sensitive soul . . . and is therefore called common, because it receiveth commonly the forms or images which the exterior senses present unto it."

In *Anatomy of Melancholy* (1621) Robert Burton described three inner senses: fantasy, memory, and common sense, "the judge or moderator of the rest." Common sense came to mean the "wisdom which is every man's inheritance." It makes us aware of "gross contradictions, palpable inconsistencies, and unmasked imposture. By a man of common sense we mean one who knows, as we say, chalk from cheese" (1726).

As a writer said in 1770,

Common sense hath, in modern times, been used by philosophers, both French and British, to signify that power of mind which perceives truth . . . not by progressive argumentation, but by an instantaneous, instinctive, and irresistible impulse, derived neither from education nor from habit, but from nature.

The word *radical* comes from the Latin *radii*, meaning "roots." In English "the radical" meant the vital juice in fruits and vegetables, and later the humors in the human body. People spoke of radical humidity, humors, moisture, sap. Soon it came to mean the essence or substance of things. In the fifteenth and sixteenth centuries radical was also "a direct source of sense."

Radical doesn't mean "far out," it means far in. When we get to the radical, we get to the essence—to the root of the problem. True common sense is body, mind, and heart, sensed in the moment.

It's time to reclaim these essential concepts of "radical" and "common sense" in tandem. There is not a more convenient term to describe multisensory perception. Data plus history plus instinct. Solutions arise out of an inner reading, a polling of our various senses reviewed in the light of experience. This sense/insight is too quick for thought. It is a gestalt, whole-seeing, whole-feeling.

We all have a capacity for common sense. Together our radical essence and common sense can become a source of knowing. Radical common sense reads all the frequencies. The senses in unison are the song of the body, and anyone who wishes can call upon this "single sense."

Like breathing, the senses are both voluntary and involuntary. To check in with common sense we have to tune in. Common sense requires that we turn down the volume of an overactive mind. Straining to make sense of things impedes the flow.

The War on Our Senses

Sometimes we overuse one sense to the detriment of the rest. Ever since the invention of the photograph in the nineteenth century, the visual sense has dominated the others. We became more and more insistent on having illustrations with stories. Kodak introduced the snapshot. Movies became the rage. Then television seized us, followed by video, cable, computer graphics, digital animation, and virtual reality.

Our taste buds take second place. Fruits and vegetables are engineered to satisfy our visual appetites, whatever the sacrifice in flavor and nutrition. Toxins of every kind assault our biochemistry. Electromagnetic radiation zaps the natural bioelectrical fields that shape us.

Air pollution and synthetic fragrances dominate our noses. Traffic, loud radios, and congested population overstimulate our hearing. Watching television, our right hemispheres have to assemble the dots into a picture. We haven't the energy left for left-brain discrimination. Heavy viewers actually become heavy; something in the habit itself slows down metabolism.

So-called "natural flavors" are natural in name only, extracted from organic materials through harsh chemical processing. "Clean-labeling," the manufacturers call it, and the Food and Drug Administration calls it okay.

Our senses have been the pawns in a foolish game. When we radicalize our common sense, our intelligence will flourish. Radical common sense chooses to remember, to know, to open up all the sensory channels and to invoke the great inner sense, the multimedia channel we call imagination.

Truth is, we're moving whether we want to or not. We're gathering our belongings, and searching our ranks for leadership. The self and the leader needed for the journey are not the same as the self and the leader who attempt to repair the past.

The wise among us are gathering their clues and directions from everywhere, even the knowledge of children and eccentrics and those with whom they disagree.

Radical common sense gives us the wherewithal to invent and reinvent, to borrow from each other, to surrender forms and tactics that no longer work, and to redesign those worth saving.

Radical common sense is both old and new. It is wisdom gleaned from experience that recognizes the perishable opportunities of the moment. It is the willingness to admit error and the refusal to be deterred by failure.

If we are to thrive as individuals, the prescription is the same as that for social renewal: the radical good sense to take leadership of ourselves. Visionaries identify with a cause that reaches beyond themselves, their family, and friends. Something bigger than personal success. "Will I make it?" leads to a more compelling question, "What should I be doing now?"

Our questions are our liberators. It's often remarked that when the student is ready the teacher will arrive. When a large enough question has been asked, the lesson plan will appear. One has said yes, I want to know. This choice can only be made by each of us individually, but it contains the seeds of a world revolution. Heroism, it becomes apparent, is nothing more than becoming our latent larger selves.

We *can* get there from here. We are a problem-solving species. When we call upon our resources we make undreamed-of leaps. The advantage we have at this moment in history is the cross-fertilization of art and science, of spirituality and science, of analysis and intuitive flashes. By pulling together the scattered threads of psychology and brain science we can tap into our radical common sense. It is the remedy for what ails us.

The journey, let us confess, is an odyssey to the core. The discoveries will be discoveries of ourselves. And there's the real challenge.

The Great Migration requires that, in fact, we become the people we always meant to be.

3 WAKING UP IN THE DARK

Vision in a Time of Paradox

We throw our hands before our eyes and cry that it is dark.

—UNKNOWN

Though night has sealed my eyes with a pair of impenetrable shades, I look for light, a little light.

—GU CHENG

Without the tempering of common sense, the rational mind is literally half-cocked, as blind in its mania for control as the superstition it scorns. Exalting the power of reason does not banish old passions and fears. Least of all does it banish mystery.

The illusion of control is based on that same old myth of predictability. Our passion for certainty grew out of a misunderstanding of science in its original sense. *Science* derives from the Latin *scientia*, knowing.

Our forebears spoke in one breath of "science and conscience." They pronounced it "con science" (with knowledge). In ancient Latin *conscientia* meant knowledge with another person. In English it came to mean "a knowledge of one's inner truths," or as the *Oxford English Dictionary* quotes, "deity in the bosom."

Science tempered by reflection is not the scientism we have deified in modern times. We've been caught in a mindless materialism that ironically threatens our material existence. We've been born into a cult that has made a god of numbers. We worship rankings, quantities, statistics, profit margins, and polls. We revere the bottom line, the top drawer, the gold-medal winner, Dow-Jones Averages, Gross Domestic Product, IQ range, Most Valuable Player, our One and Only, and the vintage year of our favorite champagne.

We want to know first, last, biggest, best, most, least, latest, and how much the baby weighs. We've mapped the genome. We captured the quark. By God or by Newton we will know.

There is something akin to superstition in this Cult of Numbers. Many rationalists are afraid of phenomena that cannot be measured. Interesting, isn't it, that the Sanskrit word *maya*, meaning "illusion," derives from the same root as *measure*?

In our zeal for final answers we have hitched our wagon to the wrong star. Our adherence to a paradigm of measurement and limits has confused our senses. Numbers, numbers, everywhere, and a crisis of values.

Descartes maintained that one could not trust one's senses. He also believed that the science of measures could lead to absolute certainty. His brilliance as a mathematician swayed the scientific community. Newton's discovery of the laws of gravity seemed to validate Descartes. When the Arabs invented the concept of zero, opening the way for mathematical precision, measurement became a holy crusade.

Little by little, measuring extended to more nebulous things, like traits and qualities. Early attempts to distinguish levels of intelligence led to the industry of IQ testing, the quotient Stephen J. Gould described as "the mismeasurement of man." Sophisticated mathematics led to the development of the "scientific method," the attempt to capture facts in a net of probabilities. Numbers stimulated other business, like polls to determine which set of number-mongers was likelier to win. Competing leaders could now fire off statistics to wound one another with volleys of numbers meant to cast the opponent as a liar or a fool.

Today we have the *Fortune* 500 companies, the *Fortune* 200, the *Fortune* 100, and so on. Countries compare notes on imports, exports, and production. Nations and states and even neighborhoods test their students and compare their scores to others. Spectator sports have promoted a cultural preoccupation with winning and losing.

Our unquestioned allegiance to the Cult of Numbers led us to the economic paradigm that says that only that which generates economic growth is worth doing. This undermines our sense of responsibility to the community, to the environment, and to our quality of life.

Common sense tells us that something is gravely amiss. If we are awake we are aware of the imbalances. But solutions are at hand, hinging on our willingness to test ourselves through personal involvement. A tremendous amount of good can be accomplished by a very few people. Miracles manifest and we make geometric leaps as we notice that it's working.

Many of us lost the light we had as children when we began to distrust our own experience and surrendered to the Cult of Numbers. A renewed faith in creativity can save the day. The ultimate in education and entertainment is to realize ourselves by signing up for the war on the root causes of all conflict and suffering—suspicion, competition for goods and honors, and a lack of attention to developing talents. By harnessing and developing our talents we reclaim our personal sovereignty.

We don't need to know exactly where we are going. It was our need for certainty that kept us in the dark. We imagined that we knew what we were doing, but many of our choices and assumptions proved wrong.

Darkness isn't danger. It's only darkness. Not a thing in and of itself, but the absence of light. All we can reasonably hope for is the inner light that can be sensed more than seen, a premonition of the good that lightens our step on the way.

The Case for Human Potential

It is humanity as a whole that is underachieving, and therein lies the crisis. We are too many, our fates are too entwined, to leave us any margin for stupidity.

We have to wake up. We have to discern the behavioral patterns and plots that make us stupid. The opposite of stupid is not
smart, but awake. The idea of perpetual awakening is not new.

Our ability to rouse from our stupor is more vital to our
future than anything on our political agendas. Radical common sense tells us that specific problems all revolve around a
few core issues:

Can we become kinder, more rational beings?

Can our intelligence be enhanced?

Can we transform our narrow goals into a bigger
picture?

Throughout history philosophers have debated the issue of
human improvability. Revolutionaries have argued that "ordinary" people are potentially smarter and better than they're
cracked up to be.

Today, when the issue of native ability is literally life and
death for our species, we have access to an immense body of scientific research. The big-picture evidence for human capacity is
direct, not circumstantial. It needs to be looked at as a whole.

Visionary science is happening. Individuals and teams of
scientists are exploring basic function, trying to understand
the meshing of brain structures and the alphabet soup of neu-
rochemicals. Others are studying the curious interface between
the material and immaterial, the mechanism whereby mental
and emotional states affect and are affected by the body.

A famous neuroscientist remarked that most researchers
"have a lot of the answers, but they don't know the questions."
There are good reasons—extreme specialization, political constraints within the profession, and a funding process that
rewards timid proposals. Researchers ask only questions to
which they're likely to have answers.

Experiments are designed, grants are written and
approved, work is performed, and findings are written up in

highly specialized journals with small readership. Frequently a single experiment is teased apart into narrow subfindings to produce multiple articles. The titles go onto the authors' resumes and enhance their professional standing. Furthermore, the laboratory environment of a scientist is too far removed from the hubbub of society to address its needs.

Flat-Earth Psychology

In the Middle Ages, sailors refused to travel beyond a certain point for fear they'd slip off the edge. In our day we have our own counterpart: Flat-Earth Psychology, a conviction about human limits.

The Flat-Earth notion of fixed intelligence can be traced to Francis Galton, cousin of Charles Darwin. Having observed that the children of violinists tended to play the violin and the sons of oarsmen became oarsmen, Galton concluded that such abilities were inherited.

Lewis Terman carried Galton's torch as the twentieth-century champion of the gene theory. Beginning in 1921 he and his colleagues followed hundreds of "gifted children" from elementary school through midlife. All the subjects had scored in the so-called "genius" range and had been recommended by their teachers, who excluded rebels and youngsters who learned unconventionally. When the Terman group was evaluated in adulthood there was virtually no incidence of creative achievement.

Terman had grossly underestimated environmental effects. Most of the children in his study had learned to read before starting school without help, their parents claimed, and Terman believed them. He assumed the children had learned to read because they were gifted, whereas their early reading gave them a leg up. What Terman found were not geniuses but children who were good test takers.

In 1903 the French Army commissioned psychologist Alfred Binet to measure the aptitude of potential recruits. Elements of

Binet's tests are present in the still-popular Stanford-Binet IQ test. Most IQ tests are based largely on speed of response, which cannot predict performance in nonacademic situations. Tests cannot assess depth or quality of thinking.

The notion of fixed intelligence is a universal error of the first magnitude. It's incorporated into our child-rearing and educational theory, the workplace, and our attitude toward the aged. It colors our expectations and strangles our ambitions. The paradigm of limits is so prevalent that we don't even think about it. Because leaps of learning and dramatic progress are not typical in our educational system, we ignore the evidence that giant steps take place. Whether in lockstep education, mandatory retirement, or the caretaking of the "hopelessly" retarded and mentally ill, these sacred-cow assumptions dictate our policies.

Fortunately, just as a handful then knew the world to be round, there are credible professionals talking about a vast evolutionary potential in human beings, even those at the low end of the IQ scale.

The evidence is there. Diet supplements increased the intelligence quotients of retarded young people so dramatically that 25 percent of them were transferred into regular classrooms.

Retarded children with IQs of 25–50 were taught sign language by a psychologist. Within a short time they could read from two hundred to four thousand words in sign language. One-third of the children were then reclassified as "educable."

Educable retarded children (IQs 50 to 75) learned to read so well using a new method that nearly half were reclassified and assigned to regular classrooms. In one study, normal or superior artistic ability was found in children who had been judged moderately or profoundly retarded on the basis of their language skills.

Even "hopeless" schizophrenia is curable. Social workers and psychiatrists in Vermont followed and counseled hundreds of chronic schizophrenics who had been released into local communities in the 1950s. Three decades later one-half to two-thirds of these "incurables" were greatly improved or fully recovered. Nearly half displayed no psychiatric symptoms at all. The most frequently cited reason for improvement was: "Somebody actually cared about me."

Two long-term European studies showed similar recovery rates. These results cast serious doubt on chronic schizophrenia as a legitimate diagnosis. A researcher speculated that psychiatrists may be biased toward "hopeless" diagnoses because they get little feedback about the success of those who were discharged. At the same time they see the deterioration of hospitalized patients.

Just as blind people have more richly developed auditory centers, combat veterans who suffered left-hemisphere injuries were found to be superior to noninjured veterans in right-hemisphere functions.

What of "normal" students? Adolescent girls in India benefited from iron supplements—a sensible regimen. English schoolchildren were more attentive when given a glucose drink in mid-afternoon. Children given light treatment for their seasonal depression didn't fall into their characteristic slumps.

Even aging need not take its customary toll. Studies have shown that the progressive fading of vision, hearing, smell, and taste does not take place in those who keep physically fit. Intelligence *increases* with age for active people. One experiment showed if there were no time constraints older people performed many tasks as well as they had forty years earlier.

The prospects are pretty heartening. In twenty years the Republic of Korea accomplished a miracle: The populace went from 90 percent illiteracy to 90 percent literacy. Korean educators attribute this to the policy decision to place first graders at the top of the national agenda.

As Tocqueville observed, a large-scale effort to educate a society is no casual undertaking. Most of us are products of the very system we hope to change—the system that undermined our confidence and turned off our enthusiasm. As individuals and as a society, we are not likely to mobilize a real effort unless the stakes are high. The stakes are high. We have to wake up, with the vision to dream.

The Freedom to Dream

I like the dreams of the future better than the history of the past.

—THOMAS JEFFERSON

Vision is radical common sense in action. An imagined goal organizes our intelligence and lights our fire. It brings forth genius and talents. Vision sees beyond the norm and the present, anticipating needs and possibilities. It gives us the ability to grasp the larger picture—the world beyond this road.

Vision is at the cutting edge of human intelligence. Throughout history our ability to think experimentally has shaped us. What distinguished our Paleolithic ancestors was their remarkable art and inventiveness.

The capacity to see the possible and how to get there is the innate mechanism for evolution and social progress. The editors of *Inc.* magazine described vision as "the ability to look at a volatile and uncertain landscape, and to see nothing but the bright colors of opportunity."

Visionary was once synonymous with *dreamer*, a person whose ideas were insubstantial and romantic. As recently as 1986 *Webster's New Collegiate Dictionary* defined visionary as one given to "impractical plans."

Half a century ago visionary was applied to religious prophets or people promoting unrealistic schemes. Visionaries were misunderstood, persecuted, rarely acknowledged in their lifetime. We praise their foresight in hindsight. Time and their great sacrifices eventually prove how practical they were. In retrospect we see that they sought answers to problems their contemporaries had not yet acknowledged.

A Hungarian obstetrician living in Vienna in the nine-teenth century saved countless women from dying of childbed fever by insisting that doctors in the hospital wash their hands before delivering babies. Ignaz Semmelweis, attacked by peers who refused to listen, eventually went insane from the pres-sure. Ironically, he died from an infected injury.

Were people like Semmelweis ahead of their time, or were their peers asleep?

Some of our pressing environmental problems and their remedies were foreseen long ago. As early as the 1950s biolo-gist Julian Huxley warned that humanity was exhausting nat-ural resources and destroying species. After World War II, when Charles Lindbergh was flying for the military, he got an aerial view of the desecration of the South Sea islands. He turned his efforts to preserving "the wildness that is the source of our cre-ativity." Chief Seattle of the Duwamish and Squamish tribes of the American Northwest warned a hundred years ago that progress was destroying the natural landscape.

The Jesuit philosopher Pierre Teilhard de Chardin wrote of "ever new eyes with ever more to see." And ever more to hear, smell, taste, and feel.

Charles Darwin described himself as less clever than his contemporaries. He was superior in only one trait—"noticing things which easily escape attention." Visionaries seem to notice what others don't see.

Einstein remarked that his slowed development afforded him time to ponder the physical world before acquiring lan-guage. When he was five years old and sick in bed his father gave him a compass. The discovery of magnetic North triggered a vision in the boy—a life-long attraction to unseen forces.

Vision enables "ordinary people" to accomplish miracles, and virtually everyone is equipped with the necessary gear. To make it through the crisis we have no choice but to cultivate vision. When we relinquish our right to envision we surrender a precious part of our liberty—the freedom to dream.

The Visionary Style

A vision suggests itself because it is possible. It requires cooperation. Vision is active but not manipulative. It's a process of
interplay between present and potential realities.

Vision includes an abstract mechanical sense, a feeling for
how things work or fail. A practiced visionary peers into the
workings of whole systems. A grasp of a situation increases the
likelihood of finding solutions. For example, student leaders
opposing the Vietnam War saw that they could have an impact
by challenging the university's investment in weapons
research. Antiapartheid leaders in the 1980s used a worldwide
boycott against South Africa.

Founded in 1998 around a single issue—opposition to the
Republican-led effort to impeach Democratic president Bill
Clinton—MoveOn.org evolved into a powerful advocacy
group with more than 1.4 million members.

The owner of a television network took pride in funding
programs on social issues. But financing was too costly.
Someone suggested he form a nonprofit organization as a
vehicle for other foundations to underwrite quality programs. The owner could run the socially relevant shows he
liked and the public-interest groups would have a forum to
air their projects.

At first he was skeptical; the idea seemed too good to be true.
Then he laughed delightedly, "Ah ... there's a twist in the system."
In motivational jargon these loopholes are called "win-win."
Someone with an experimental turn of mind moves elements in
mental space until there is a fit that benefits all parties.

Someone once remarked that you can hold a real solution
up to the light, and it will work from every angle. That's how
you know when you're on the right track.

4
THE SELVES WE TRAVEL WITH

The Repertory Company

In every corner of my soul there is an altar to a different god.

—FERNANDO PESSOA

One of the most harmful illusions that can beguile us is the belief that we are indivisible, immutable, totally consistent beings.

—PIERO FERRUCCI

When we're preparing for a long and arduous journey we generally think in terms of food and supplies. Rarely do we check for the real essentials—our wits, our self-understanding, our enthusiasm, and endurance. These can keep us going long after the rations have run out.

Under yon pinyon tree is a rock, and under the rock is a secret: Beware of the assumptions that you make about other people. They're often a mystery to themselves, so don't imagine that you can read them. Little by little we all fall into the trap of imputing bad motives, and the more we do it the more seductive it becomes. It's a simpler explanation than the truth.

Since we will never know the deepest secrets of another, our best shot at understanding life still comes from probing the mysteries of our own hearts. Here we find an occasional nugget, an insight that makes us suspect that somewhere there's a vein of gold.

Once in a while we undertake a task that calls upon resources we didn't know we had. Where were these powers lurking? As Thomas Paine pointed out, we seem to develop new senses and capacities as they are needed. Is there no limit? Why, then, do we coast until there's an emergency?

Vision ups the ante. Having carried out a difficult task or two, we become familiar with challenges and more willing to meet the next one. We meet new parts of ourselves.

When we're migrating to a new understanding, we call upon "traveling skills"—a sense of adventure, the courage to take off into parts unknown, and the imagination to conceive of ourselves again and again. It's as if a whole company were traveling within each of us.

And where have they been, these states and skills? Untapped, you might say, but that raises another question: Why? How is it that we don't call on these assorted abilities in our normal range of activities?

People who live in remote places are versatile out of necessity. They can't delegate healing to a doctor, education to a school, or decisions to a bureaucrat. They have to build, feed themselves, and keep up their spirits without benefit of clergy or therapist.

When we collectively began to assign various functions to specialists, you might say we typecast ourselves. It seemed efficient. Experts would know more about their subject than generalists ever could. Perfect each role, people thought, and we will have a more perfect society.

The problem is that life isn't designed that way. Biology, chemistry, archeology, anthropology, and psychology have no separate existence in the natural world. They are waves and currents in a sea of being.

If specialists saw their territory as part of a system they could be more responsive to change. If they kept their minds open to opportunities for transformation we would have a series of self-organizing systems that pass information along their various currents to inform the whole.

With no cause requiring commitment, the idle warrior degenerates into a grump, a troublemaker, or "a rebel without a clue." If we ignore our body signals because the doctor can't find what's wrong, our inner physician may take an early retirement. We give up singing because we can't compare with the professionals, we "can't draw a straight line" so why deny our artist self. The experts speak, and the inner counsel grows silent.

Two Brains Across, Three Brains Deep

A major reason for our inability to dramatically educate and improve ourselves lies in our misconception about the nature of the self. When we operate from a simplistic paradigm, we shouldn't wonder at our lack of success.

There is considerable evidence that much of our intelligence is unconscious and therefore not easily accessible. A great many culture scouts, seminal thinkers representing a number of disciplines—neuroscience, artificial intelligence, psychiatry, psychology, and philosophy—have been sending back remarkably similar reports from their various frontiers.

Human beings are multiplex—literally, braided from many strands. The idea of a single self may be little more than a useful convention, necessary for the purpose of formal agreements and Rolodex cards.

Our views, reasons, and responses alter from time to time because multiplicity is inherent in nature, not because there is a single "I" who is somehow inconsistent.

Most thoughtful people already acknowledge that they're at least somewhat dual, an admission helped along by research on the differing behaviors of the brain's left and right hemispheres. We now take for granted that we have at least two brains.

Viewed a little differently, the brain, like ancient Gaul, is divided into three parts. The "triune brain," as described by neuroscientist Paul MacLean, is composed of three structures that evolved somewhat independently at different times. They are (1) the ancient reptilian brain, (2) the more recent neomammalian or limbic brain, and (3) the still newer neo-cortex (the hemispheres). The three parts are as yet imperfectly integrated, an unfortunate situation he calls "schizophysiology."

These three brains differ in structure, chemistry, and evolutionary history. As MacLean puts it, we are obliged to look at the world through the eyes of three quite different mentalities. To complicate things further, two of the brains, the reptilian and the limbic, appear to lack the power of speech.

One of our human biases is to imagine that that which is most recent is best. But the two older brains, although mute, are more conscious than we had imagined. They are very much present, if not accounted for.

The reptilian brain drives our habitual machinery, making change somewhat difficult. By always reverting to precedent, the reptilian brain is responsible for apparently irrational behavior. Anatomists have unfairly blamed such behavior on the limbic brain, seat of the emotions. In other words, some of our periodic nonsense is triggered by instinct or habit.

The famous human resistance to new ideas, our unusual reluctance to change an intellectual construct, can be blamed on our maintainer, the reptilian self. According to Paul MacLean and his triune brain theory, this ancient brain is a traditionalist, "a slave to precedent . . . neurosis-bound by an ancestral super-ego."

Animal experiments show that the oldest brain structure reacts to shadows or "phantoms," partial representation of stimuli—a dark blur or peripheral flash. "An incomplete stimulus can set off elaborate, even ritualistic behavior," MacLean said. We all recall incidents when we were startled by a misheard remark or alarmed by what we thought we saw.

Impressions, illusions, and half-truths play in the theater of our minds. Social ills are caused in part by our attempts to force the two older brains to match the pace and planning of the new brain. Psychosomatic disease, alcoholism, and addiction may originate in the automatic thinking and behaving of the reptilian brain.

Whether we are thrill seekers or stay-at-homes, gregarious or withdrawn, eager for change or fiercely stuck, depends a great deal on the dynamics of our brains. Shy people have lower than normal levels of dopamine, the transmitter associated with novelty seeking.

The Multiplex Self

A fruitful new way of seeing right and left, a turn on the theoretical spiral, is emerging from research done by Richard Davis and collaborators at various institutions. Davis has determined that the left hemisphere mediates positive emotions, whereas the right processes unpleasant feelings.

The two hemispheres seem to operate as a kind of guidance system, one urging approach and the other withdrawal. We are attracted and repelled, consciously or unconsciously, as we go about our business.

Given that hemispheric dominance for certain functions switches every ninety minutes or so, we can better understand the revolving door of our yeses and noes. Most of us do not wake up married to strangers, but we change enough over several hours or days that our close friends could identify a whole roster of characters, each of them unarguably "me"—the peaceful one, the uptight one, the child, the thinker, the radical, the conservative, and so on.

There are ten-minute crossover periods during the transition that provide a chance for input into the mysterious system.

It's easier to notice these shifts in others, of course. Think of those you know well. Even if they are fairly consistent, you can still detect configurations, selves distinct in their confidence levels and energy. Sometimes we even seek companions to match our most intimate "present company." When we're feeling deeply discouraged, we're more likely to seek the company of a quiet or mildly depressed person ("misery loves company"), whereas a slightly "down" feeling can send us to a radiant friend who tends to lift our spirits.

There is a relatively confident, energetic self who makes commitments that horrify the self who has to carry them out. The celebratory Saturday night self has little truck with the Sunday morning zombie. We vary, of course, in our repertory companies, but we all have them. Learning to detect the shifts, especially sudden alterations, is key to self-understanding.

Learning to activate these shifts is essential to self-management.

Each of Us Is a Crowd

The timid self forgets what the confident self knows. The busy self overlooks promises made by the peace-at-any-price self.

In other words, although I may tell a therapist or friend that I wish to control or change a certain behavior, my misbehaving self may not be present when I do. The wisdom apparently gained may remain hidden from the me that needs to change—unless I am clever at reminding all of the me's in my environment. The me who vows not to overeat is not the same one who rationalizes an extra wedge of cake.

As psychiatrists John and Helen Watkins put it:

> We are semi-united states. We have organized segments or regions that have local control. Consideration must be given to states' rights as well as to the national welfare if we are to help people organize their multiplicities into coherent unities.

In each of us there may be an athlete, a scholar, a nurturing parent, and so on. Our facial musculature, gestures, vocabulary, accents, handwriting, phobias, and even our memories may be versatile in ways we've never dreamed of.

Our stream of consciousness includes the stream of selves.

Recognizing our variable states is a giant step toward self-realization.

Remember the words of an old campfire song, "When your friends are my friends, and my friends are your friends—the more we get together, the happier we'll be." The same might be said of our different selves with their different values. Each—conservative, daring, lazy, ambitious—must be recognized if we are to facilitate inner agreement.

"Each of us is a crowd," Florentine psychiatrist Piero Ferrucci said. Ferrucci is a practitioner of psychosynthesis, a technique developed by Italian psychiatrist Roberto Assagioli, that aims at integrating the conflicting energies of various sub-psyches—the perfectionist, the whining child, the procrastinator, the dictator.

Surely it is one of our great puzzlements and humiliations that others accuse us of inconsistency. At the same time we are frustrated by the changeability in others, their apparent amnesia for things they clearly implied or did.

Competing selves cannot be held in check for an indefinite period, according to Douglas Hofstadter's *Metamagical Themas*.

> They cannot be clamped down, forbidden to act. Each inner voice is in actuality composed of millions of smaller parts, each active. Under the proper circumstance, those small activities will someday all point in the same direction, and at that moment each inner voice will crystallize, will undergo a phase transition, will emerge from obscurity and proclaim itself an active member of the community of selves.

Hofstadter is saying that each new identity—for example, the brand-new gardening self of a person who claimed to have a "black thumb"—wishes to be recognized. "It may attempt to seize power," Hofstadter says. He cites as an example his own piano-playing subself who, given the floor, "refuses to relinquish it for hours on end."

Collaboration Among the Selves

Psychiatrist John Beahrs insists that psychology itself is hampered by a failure to recognize the simple fact of multiplicity. He offers a "co-consciousness theory" of human functioning: When people seem to violate good sense the multiple selves are in conflict.

Two may be evenly matched, thus paralyzing action, or one may be sabotaging the efforts of many. Furthermore, if such struggles remain unconscious, they have a cumulative effect on society. C. G. Jung insisted that when people are unaware of their inner opponents, the world acts out the conflicts and is torn into warring communities.

It's important to concede that we are all at least covertly multiple, and a good thing, too. Those who are doggedly the same day in and day out are probably as bored as they are boring. Ralph Waldo Emerson once remarked that "a foolish consistency is the hobgoblin of little minds." Our obliviousness to these selves, not our multiplicity, is the problem.

In Beahr's view, the personality expressing itself as "I" at the moment—the self in the driver's seat—can be unaware of information known to another sub-personality. Behavior we call unconscious may be a conscious choice of one of the parts. "Each component of the psyche is not just an abstract mechanism but an experiencing being that we can contact and communicate with."

Visionaries learn to use this multiplicity creatively.

As Beahrs puts it, "The unconscious is not a cauldron of fury crying for expression but . . . the source of all life and growth." Versatility of expression enables us to respond appropriately, acting like an experienced general when there's a need to take charge, or soft and motherly when such traits are called for, and playful when the spirit of play is abroad.

The Society of Mind

Comedian Tommy Smothers used to refer to "my brother and my selves." Thinking of "my selves" rather than "myself" resolves a few mysteries. In fact, the array of selves may reflect the measure of our genius.

Marvin Minsky, an artificial intelligence specialist at MIT, sees these subselves as a configuration of specialized brain functions—a society of agents capable of cooperating on our behalf. If we are ever to quantify intelligence shrewdly enough to detect qualitative differences between individuals, Minsky says, we may find that it correlates with how many of these agents an individual has vying for attention at the same time.

This mind-boggling notion opens us up to vast creative possibilities. Intelligence may reflect a company of talented subselves, each at the ready with a skill or insight. Our ability to manage these perspectives and passions rewards us with inner and outer balance.

The eighteenth-century philosopher Emanuel Swedenborg correlated high functioning with an abundance of inner communities with "constituents." The more communities and the more members within a community, Swedenborg wrote in *Arcana Coelestia*, the better.

> [P]erfection and strength come from a harmonious gathering of many constituents, which act as one. . . . It is not just one community that flows into a given organ or member but many, and . . . there are many individuals in each community.

South African statesman Jan Smuts predicted in 1926 that the individual is going to be universalized, and

> the universal is going to be individualized, and thus from both directions the whole is going to be enriched.

Plasticity, freedom, creativeness are necessary for the new groupings and structures which are to arise on the psychic level.

In Minsky's model, consciousness is that aspect of the mind specialized for knowing how to use the other, more hidden systems. Seeing our minds as societies could help explain why it is hard for us to adopt new ideas. Minsky's "Investment Principle" says that the oldest ideas have advantages over those that come later:

The earlier we learn a skill, the more methods we . . . acquire for using it. Each new idea must then compete, all unprepared, against a mass of skills the old ideas have accumulated. That's why it's almost always easier to do new things in old ways instead of starting fresh. Each new idea, however good in principle, seems alien and awkward until we master it.

The administrative brain learns to label and organize its specialized functions. For a child to become unusually smart, Minsky suggests, the administrative brain must experience a "lucky accident" that calls attention to the learning process itself. If we're lucky or observant, we will eventually notice the accidental nature of learning. From that point, we can take advantage of these "accidents."

To restate: It is neither possible nor desirable to bring everything into consciousness, but we can greatly enlarge our spiritual, mental, and emotional worlds if we simply remember that we are profoundly influenced by transactions outside the range of awareness. Our less assertive selves, set at ease by our admission, can deliver their messages with less conflict and greater clarity.

Human Necessity

Personality is not the same as self. Personality is not so much who we are as it is an embodied story—our reading of life's trials and consolations, our teachers and meetings and partings.

Personality is largely based on perceived realities. Naturally, society, a mingling of numberless perceived realities, lacks coherence. Certain values are proclaimed but not lived by.

Although we say that honesty is the best policy, we tend to practice a kind of defensive dishonesty. The seller asks more than he expects to receive because the buyer is going to offer less than he expects to pay.

Because we're afraid that others won't grasp the importance of what we're saying, we exaggerate. At the same time, since we know that "everybody exaggerates," we doubt each other. Fudging in big and little ways, we lose our sensitivity to the lie. Disinformation has become the diet of the day.

Having delegated our social responsibilities to the mysterious Them—the institutions—we become increasingly disenchanted with the job they are doing. Seeing little stewardship of the common interest, we become cynical. We care less, know less, do less. We resist being taxed for reforms, yet we are not inclined to help directly. We escape. We cocoon. Our schools, our health care, our esthetics, our environment, and our economy spiral downward.

It could be argued that the culprit is greed—the avarice of those who misuse, bribe, monopolize, steal, hoard, and extort. Since antisocial behaviors are prevalent we can easily see ourselves as victims and feel paralyzed.

People generally agree that something must change. What is that something? It makes no sense to look to the guardians of the status quo for solutions or to the exploiters for a change of heart. Antisocial patterns are dissolved neither by arguments nor preaching. Despite laws and punishments, despite social mores, our world is neither just nor balanced.

Imbalances within ourselves perpetuate the misguided habits that manifest as our current world crises. In *The Development of Personality*, Jung pointed out that

> no one develops his personality because somebody tells
> him it would be useful or advisable to do so. Nature has

never yet been taken in by well-meaning advice. The only thing that moves nature is causal necessity, and that goes for human nature, too. Without necessity nothing budges, the human personality least of all.

Jung called the personality "tremendously conservative." The developing personality obeys no caprice or command, only brute necessity.

Starting now we can refuse to accept the unacceptable. Wherever we are, whatever our skills and status, we can begin. The tricky part is that we have to work on ourselves, our subselves, and our surroundings at the same time.

We can ask: What is it in me that unsettles my conscience? What are my habits, and how do I rationalize them? What do I have to do to become a better or more well-rounded individual?

If we find it difficult to change ourselves we can hardly expect society to change. Society, in other words, is a collection of people all too much like us. But we can fight fire with fire. Rather than struggling to overthrow the inner bureaucracy we can use our automating mechanisms to create—and reinforce—positive patterns of behavior.

New Habits, New Selves

We often describe ourselves as "creatures of habit." Other than habit, we'd have no way of establishing automatic behaviors and thus would have no time to reflect or create. We'd be too busy putting one foot in front of the other. Hierarchies of habits get us through the day. Micro-habits are the building blocks of patterns and, eventually, personalities.

It helps to imagine cooperation among our brain regions and a new kind of harmony between subselves. Our biochemistry may influence us to be foolhardy, cowardly, or rigid. Yet we can modulate those drives into exploration, vigilance, and good housekeeping.

Edna O'Brien, the Irish novelist, described having fifteen people locked inside, and they all fit. Occasionally, we can still the crowd completely, according to Lewis Thomas:

> The only way to quiet them down, get them to stop, is to play music. That does it. Bach stops them every time, in their tracks, almost as though that's what they've been waiting for.

After a decade of research, William James said that the only thing he knew for sure about the human brain is that it is excellent at forming habits. The only strategy that makes sense is to create good habits.

On-the-Job Training

We make more progress on the job than in merely contemplating our sins or in studying how to improve ourselves. Personal change—the stripping away of unnecessary behaviors and beliefs—happens best when we're apprenticing ourselves to a worthwhile task. Even menial jobs train us to persist and be patient and give us the chance to excel. Once we learn excellence in simple tasks we acquire a kind of jet propulsion— our own higher standards.

We gear up for Life, not just a living. Everything matters. Setbacks, emotional ups and downs, become part of an epic journey.

There are no overnight successes. To succeed means to go through a series of steps.

As we feel more engaged it is easier to see how our collective life could be improved. Techniques are not enough. Without the inner suspicion that we can transform our basic way of doing business, we are merely "sewing wings on caterpillars."

As the inner selves join forces we see better how working principles work together. These understandings are self-propagating, like DNA, germinating and multiplying, ready for the next encounter.

This sense of forward movement, this blossoming of our capacities, becomes part of our casual conversation. Just as we've been operating from a certain sense of "should" and "probably won't," one day soon our many selves will come from "can"—and "will."

In the pages to come we will meet various selves face to face, allies that correspond to the multiplicity of our being. They can come forth singly or together.

We will explore and ponder their potential qualities. Modern science and ancient wisdom, heroic testimonials and historic examples, will help reveal the visionaries' secret technology. We aren't stuck with our acquired personalities or resigned to just one "calling."

As the research at hand sheds a brighter light on the mysterious nature of our being, a new and powerful capacity for change unfolds. We realize that our failed attempts at wholeness merely reflect a failure to embrace the tapestry of characters woven within each of us.

If we tame our fear of the community within us we can consciously evolve the functions of our higher subselves. If we're to find our true companions and allies in the world it helps to gather together first the tribe of our inner elect.

5

CHALLENGE AND THE ART OF SELF-ENCOURAGEMENT

The Athlete

Souls are like athletes that need opponents worthy of them if they are to be tried and extended and pushed to the full use of their powers and rewarded according to their capacity.

—THOMAS MERTON

You work best when the wind is against you.

—SWEDISH PROVERB

If we are to achieve our goals and dreams, we have to stretch. We have to rise to the occasion. Excellence, in this sense, is not an achievement or a luxury; it is oxygen to a drowning soul. The notion of a status quo is an illusion. Nothing stands still. As individuals or as societies, we are healing or degenerating, moving toward life or toward death.

Folk wisdom has a lot to say about the value of working our way through difficulty, of taking on more than we think we can handle. We talk about having undergone "a trial by fire," of being tempered, of "the school of hard knocks." In the Chinese idiom one is said to "embrace the tiger."

From childhood on we have all heard, and often resented, the counsel that our greatest learning comes from difficulty. Most of us keep wishing that understanding will come easily, later, when we "have our act together."

Score one for traditional wisdom. Judging from the scientific evidence, challenge is the brain's wake-up call. If something doesn't seize our attention, our brains tend to operate in an indifferent way. A lack of stimulation—boredom—may even be a major cause of illness.

Study the lives of exceptional people, and you are struck by one fact: a disproportionate number suffered misfortune early in life. In some cases it was a tragedy, in others a physical handicap, poverty, extreme emotional sensitivity, or a learning problem such as a reading disability. The traits they developed to compensate for their handicaps proved useful in other ways.

Pitcher Jim Abbott, who was breaking records for the then Anaheim Angels as a twenty-one-year-old rookie, has no right hand. As soon as Abbott let go of the pitch, he switched his glove to his left hand in defense. This extra training of his reflexes may well have helped him as a pitcher.

It becomes ever more evident that so-called giftedness is actually a talent for using one's abilities. We might call it the gift of being gifted.

This talent for identifying and using one's gifts, interestingly, seems to derive from having developed any ability—no matter which—to its edge. The practice of developing ability is fundamental. Through this, and not through talent alone, we become able people.

Developing an ability to our utmost leads to an experimental attitude. Once we've mastered the knack of mastering ourselves—of applying ourselves, persisting, and re-inspiring ourselves—we can master many things. Each new language acquired makes the next one easier to learn. Our brains generalize, building on previous knowledge and discovering the common threads.

Once we have overcome a specific obstacle, all obstacles become less threatening. Once we have endured great pain to reach a goal, all pain becomes more endurable. Each attainment is a bootstrap. Each effort adds to our expertise, which in turn generates the confidence to assault new mountains.

Olympic swimmer Janet Evans remarked that she often won when behind in the stretch. "I always have good finishes. You go as hard as you can until the end unless you're dying. You can always rest when it's over."

Her father said, "People always told her that she couldn't swim fast because she was so little. Maybe she's always tried to prove to people that she could."

Challenge stimulates the brain and provokes action. The more we attempt, the more we see patterns and analogies. We begin to grasp principles. Whereas we were once striving to overcome a handicap—poor reading, lack of coordination, always being "the new kid" in school, poverty—now we're well prepared for more than coping.

Six Inches at a Time

Some of the achievements of severely handicapped people are not merely inspiring, not just humbling. They take your breath away.

A fifty-year-old blind man walked the length of the Appalachian Trail, more than two thousand miles, crossing fourteen states, accompanied only by his guide dog. He broke a rib along the way, and he nearly drowned in an icy river, but he had no regrets. He fulfilled his purpose, to show his faith in God.

Using a special T-bar device a twenty-nine-year-old paraplegic spent eight days pulling himself up the sheer granite face of El Capitan in Yosemite National Park. "You have a dream," he said, "and you know the only way that dream is going to happen is if you just do it—even if it's six inches at a time."

After ten years of helping with the Special Olympics, an Oregon woman wondered if the mentally retarded might have untapped dramatic talent. She wrote a nativity play for a group of retarded young adults. Within four years they were performing the challenging *My Fair Lady*.

Physical anomalies, although we may curse them, also create opportunities. Folk wisdom has it that "What doesn't kill you makes you strong." The endurance and resourcefulness demanded by an affliction can hardly help but ennoble us in some way.

Literature is full of such stories, perhaps because survivors want to tell their stories. They want to pass along what they have learned, and writing is something that can be done even if you are in a wheelchair, even if you are deaf and blind like Helen Keller, even if you are unable to use your hands, like Christy Brown, author of *My Left Foot*. The poor vision of Aldous Huxley, the stammer of Somerset Maugham, the epilepsy that seized Lewis Carroll—these were transmuted in their art. Tchaikovsky, Julius Caesar, Alexander the Great, Dostoevsky, and the Apostle Paul were all epileptic.

A world champion gymnast, Dmitri Bilozerchev, shattered his leg in a car accident. Five years later he regained the world title with a steel bar in his leg. Champion cyclist Lance Armstrong beat the odds and survived cancer. He then returned to racing and won the Tour de France an unprecedented seven times. A former bantam-weight Golden Gloves boxer, Mike Adame, painfully crippled by spinal meningitis, devoted himself to coaching local youths in a program to combat gang activity.

In truth such stories are not so much about gymnastics or boxing. Bilozerchev's coach said, "If Dima is remembered for only medals, it will be a shame. It was his charge to raise the sport to the next level." Adame said his real agenda is not to turn his young Latino charges into boxers. He wants to get them beyond their cultural stereotypes, off the street, and thinking about college. "One day they're going to wake up and realize they don't need boxing, that they can walk away from the ring and still be a man."

This is the gift of a prepared attitude. Physical fitness and experience are not necessarily the most important factors even in such predicaments as being stranded at sea or in the wilderness. Often the sole survivor of a disaster is an apparently fragile woman or older person who had a strong will or faith, whereas their more seasoned companions gave up hope and life.

Focus on Abilities

Individuals with handicaps typically express the wish that others would focus on their abilities, not their disabilities. A college student with a severe hearing loss pointed out that being disabled is an integral part of the human experience. "Every one of us, if we live long enough, will get age spots and lose our hearing and eyesight."

Jim Abbott said after pitching a no-hit game, "Everyone is dealt a problem in life. Mine is missing four fingers." Gale Devers, once so disabled by Graves disease that it was thought she would never walk again, set a world record in the hundred meter sprint in the Olympics to win the title, "the fastest woman in the world." Mario Lemieux, a hockey legend, and Jeff Blatnick, an Olympic gold medallist in Greco-Roman wrestling, each came back to their sports after they had been diagnosed with Hodgkins' disease. Wilma Rudolph, three times an Olympic gold medalist in track, walked with the aid of a leg brace as a child. She had double pneumonia at four, then scarlet fever, then a mild version of polio. Her memory of early childhood was of being ill and bedridden.

Violinist Itzhak Perlman, jazz pianist Michel Petrucciani, and operatic tenor Seung-Won Choi performed despite being crippled. Petrucciani remarked that his disease, a bone disorder that also stunted his growth, was a blessing because it stimulated his childhood ambition to become a jazz musician of the first order. "I have direction without the ambivalence that hinders some artists," he said. His wife said of his condition, "It shortened his childhood and made him deal with pain in a way few people understand, and it made him cherish things others take for granted."

A group of adolescents blind from birth scored significantly higher than their sighted peers on a test of imagination. The psychologist who conducted the study pointed out that blind children depend more on other senses, "including imagination." In a group of nursing-home patients, originality in art was correlated with the severity of brain damage.

Handicaps are, in fact, normal.

Engaging the Whole Brain

"The brain is meant to be challenged," neuroscientist Jerre Levy said. "Challenges are what appear to engage the whole brain, generate excitement, and provide the substrate for optimal learning."

Challenge awakens emotional commitment and motivation, and commands attention—"the highly integrated brain in action," Levy calls it. Research on split-brain patients shows that overall attention is poor when only one hemisphere is engaged. The great men and women of history, in Levy's view, are characterized *more by their attraction to challenge than by superior intellect.*

Let's consider again the idea that each of us is a community of selves, assorted functions, views and subpersonalities that inhabit our bodies. During business as usual the selves are somewhat fragmented. But if we are confronted by a challenge of sufficient magnitude, either a problem or a chosen undertaking, the inner dissension gives way to a more unified self. The elements of our personality are frightened or inspired into solidarity, just as the members of any group tend to close ranks when threatened from the outside.

And remember, too, Marvin Minsky's startling notion that our intelligence may be reckoned by the number of subselves competing for center stage. If so, presenting our selves with a challenge might engage their collective interest.

The Window of Challenge

Learning is most efficient when we are doing something hard enough to keep us on our toes but not overwhelming. This optimal window of challenge changes. When we are new at an enterprise, the simplest task can keep us alert and interested. A musical beginner can be challenged just by playing the scales. But as soon as we achieve mastery we require a new demand if we are not to become bored.

To detect the window of challenge in life we have to know when we are working *at, above,* or *below* our skill level. That means identifying the boredom in our lives, especially if it has become the norm.

The origin of *bore,* meaning an uninteresting person, is unknown. The word first appeared in print in 1766. The term *boredom,* i.e., the state of being bored, did not come into usage until 1852. The French *ennui* suggests both weariness and dissatisfaction. Boredom sometimes translates into alienation, a more political term, as in workers alienated by the repetitiveness of the assembly-line. But it all adds up to the same thing and is best exemplified by the bumper stickers that say "I'D RATHER BE SKIING" or sailing, or spelunking. In other words, "I'd rather not be here."

Boredom, a kind of withdrawal of our presence, is both painful and universal. Children and teenagers often complain that they have nothing to do, and when their parents suggest activities, they say, "Bor-ing." Parents, stumped for solutions, become bored in turn. Bored students turn into dropouts. Marriages dissolve. Workers lose interest in their jobs. Governments rise and fall because so many of us are too uninterested or too alienated to vote.

Even busy people can find their lives boring. Boredom doesn't mean having nothing to do. We can feel alienated by pointless rounds of activity.

In our time boredom is more or less taken for granted. As an ailment, it has no glamour and arouses little compassion. It's hard to imagine a charity concert or a marathon to benefit the bored. Yet boredom can be excruciating, and, according to one researcher, it can even be terminal.

A visionary artist-writer said, "When I find things I'm afraid of, I get involved right away." An artist-entrepreneur stated her policy: "When I realize I'm going to have to change, I do the hardest thing first." To overcome her fear of simple intimacy she undertook to learn contact dancing, a form inspired by the martial art aikido.

Robert Jarvik, who pioneered the artificial heart, said, "Work on the hardest, most important problem to which your talents apply. And do it for yourself. Work for the feeling that you are alive and that you are part of it all."

"If you don't invent challenges for yourself," Jessica Lange said, "acting can become boring."

The natural enjoyment that fuels a successful society depends on the dynamic match between skills and task. But, of course, challenge is in the perception. Colin Wilson told of finding himself with a stack of photocopying to do. "It seemed like half an hour out of my life, a loss. Then I realized that I could make something out of it. So I doubled my attention. I became really involved in the copying job. And I felt extraordinary." The next day, faced with another tedious task, he applied the same tactic, a deliberate focusing of attention on the job at hand. Again he found a miraculous surge of energy.

Boredom as a Cause of Illness

If we see life as an interesting challenge we are likelier than our more cynical, timid, or depressed friends to maintain our health over time. A loss of interest in one's work or surroundings often precedes illness.

Because we become adept at and accustomed to the familiar, the restless mind-body system seeks novelty. When tasks or a lifestyle become automatic, the resulting boredom produces too little energy to sustain health. In *The Psychobiology of Cancer*, Augustin de la Pena, head of psychophysiology at the Veterans Administration Hospital in Austin, Texas, proposed that each of us has a certain information-processing capacity. If we under-use our mental and emotional capacities, our physiological system goes into decline.

The body's remarkable ability to maintain itself is called homeostasis. As de la Pena sees it, homeostasis is more a matter of maintaining the same level of processing efficiency, not necessarily the same input. He suggests that we also maintain a kind of *cognitive* homeostasis, a characteristic level of information processing. If a mentally active person becomes benumbed, for whatever reason—retirement, too many disconnected details, an emotional setback—the central processing system cannot maintain its homeostasis. The more complex a cognitive structure, the greater the importance of novelty and challenge.

Children are excited by experiences that are boring or habitual to adults. The first snow of winter is an adventure to a child. The increasing incidence of cancer with age, de la Pena suggests, may not be due solely to degenerating immune mechanisms. It may also reflect increasing boredom—the feeling of "Here we go again" or "I've seen it all before."

Building a Better Brain

Our societies have been lax in facilitating intelligence from cradle to grave. This surely is the costliest of errors, greater than any of our technological or policy boondoggles.

Yet the tide can be turned at any time. Research shows that stimulation alters the brains of adult rats as well as pups. In fact, when adult rats were placed in an interesting setting, their brains began producing substances *usually found only during early development*. Even very old rats performed like pups in swimming endurance tests. "Some brain connections," the researchers said, "may be turned on (or turned up) permanently as a result of novel experiences."

These and other findings tend to support Ashley Montagu's theory of neoteny, the idea that an extended childhood or maturation period enhances intelligence in a species. Human young have the most prolonged maturation of all earthly creatures.

Stimulation actually delays the onset of aging. "Use it or lose it," said Berkeley neuroscientist Marian Diamond. To Diamond the activities that keep enhancing a rat's nervous system, even into its old age, are comparable to the interested minds we see in active elders. "Such people love life and they love others." Love and enthusiasm are signs of an engaged brain.

There is no automatic ceiling on intelligence. A long-range Seattle study monitors and measures the mental abilities of people every seven years so that it can compare the changes within individuals. People who had led challenging lives when they were middle-aged remained stable or actually showed improvement in mental abilities after age sixty. Those who did not have stimulating lives in their middle years tended to decline markedly. Older people who remain physically active tend to hear and see better than their age-mates.

The pioneering animal experiments by Diamond and her colleagues at the University of California, Berkeley, demonstrated that the brain indeed changes in response to stimulation. A rat reared in an "enriched environment" has a significantly thicker cortex than its unstimulated littermates. It also shows a 10 percent increase in a particular brain enzyme and a 10 percent increase in the number of support cells.

What sort of environment stimulates a rat? Large cages with other rat pups for playmates, and playthings like wheels, boxes, tubes, and balls. Objects to climb on, sniff, and crawl under. In the Berkeley laboratories the toys are changed twice a week. Otherwise, the rats become bored, just as we would, and their brain development is not enhanced.

In the decades since the first reports from Berkeley, laboratories all over the world have found that a stimulating environment produces extensive brain changes and superior learning in rats. By housing their rats in double-decker cages Swiss experimenters obtained a 16 percent gain in cortical thickness.

Human handling also makes the rat pups smarter and bolder. Handled females are better mothers. Handled rats are more resistant to disease and the effects of stress.

Stimulation has long-lasting effects. Very brief handling of rats during the first three weeks of life prevented later age-related deficits. *When the handled rats were old they showed almost none of the usual impairment and loss of brain cells.*

Brain stimulation of an animal benefits its offspring as well. Marian Diamond has found that stimulation affects the non-enriched pups of the experimental rats, and *their* pups, *even when the animals are reared by foster mothers.*

Diamond calls the phenomenon "enriching heredity." Such pups are heavier than normal at birth and have larger brains. In the Berkeley experiments, each succeeding generation had thicker cortices and higher birth weights than normal although only the original mothers were enriched! In Japanese experiments, the pups of enriched mothers were also superior at learning mazes.

If stimulation makes rats and their offspring smarter and stronger, what of us? These studies imply that an interested mind is an express lane to ability, both for us and for our descendants.

Psychologist Leslie Hart emphasizes that school should be vivid, like life. Input should be increased tenfold, "not by more orderly verbal lesson plans but by random, multi-channel experience! Schools could be brain-compatible rather than brain antagonistic."

The Zone of Proximal Development

In a way, an appropriate challenge is a compliment to the learner, an invitation to step up to another level of understanding. Mihaly Csikszentmihalyi, author of *Flow: The Psychology of Optimal Experience,* and his associates at the

University of Chicago report that appropriate challenge generates a sense of flow, of unselfconscious pleasure. If we come to grips with a task just beyond our present level of competence, we experience enjoyment.

In the model of mediated learning proposed by the Russian psychologist Lev Vygotsky, an older or more advanced person offers whatever help is necessary to bring another up a level in a skill or concept. The good mediator—parent, teacher, leader—is ever sensitive to the learner's readiness to move on.

The best learning, Vygotsky said, takes place *in advance of present ability*. In other words, in the face of appropriate challenge. In those areas in which our learning has not been mediated, our capacity is unknown. This unknown area—the Zone of Proximal Development, or ZPD—represents an individual's real potential to learn a specific ability.

Each of us has areas of ability and areas of ignorance. If a person has not had the benefit of specific instruction, we cannot judge his or her potential. For obvious reasons the ZPD—the untapped potential—tends to be larger in the disadvantaged. Children reared in large families or extreme poverty are unlikely to have experienced mediated learning in the home. Their caregivers may not have known what to do or were too busy trying to survive.

A lucky few are given home coaching in how to reason, to generalize, to map, to tackle difficult tasks. Only the most exceptional classroom teacher can begin to offer the resources of a "mediating" family.

Mediated learning works dramatically. Reuven Feuerstein adapted Vygotsky's ZPD for his "instrumental enrichment" method teaching retarded youngsters in Israel. They blossomed.

Children kept behind in elementary school are likelier than other students to drop out before finishing high school—not because they're stupid but because they are bored. The most effective way to ensure that they stay in school is to place them in an accelerated program so they catch up to their peers by the time they enter junior high school.

Inspired by a model program in Dade County, Florida, inner-city children in Los Angeles learned to speak Chinese, Japanese, and Russian. One hundred eighty youngsters, kindergarten through fifth grade, learned the languages using movement, nursery rhymes, and songs. They did three hours of homework a day.

Parents and teachers talk about being moved to tears by the children's progress and the pride they take in their new-found ability. "These kids will be bi-lingual and tri-lingual" one teacher said. "Instead of beating the bushes looking for work the jobs will come to them."

A teacher of German said, "The children in other schools could do much more than they are. It's only that they aren't chal-lenged enough." The overall test scores of the children in the Florida program have been among the highest in their district.

Low-income teenagers in Houston, participants in a federal summer jobs program, were asked for ideas about improving educational achievement. A tenth grader said, "The schools aren't demanding enough. If they pushed the students harder and showed why it matters they'd find more interest in school."

Vygotsky maintained that all higher psychological processes originate as social processes, something shared between people, particularly between children and adults. Most societies have given relatively little thought to latent potential or to the interpersonal side of learning.

This, then, is the catch. If we have not been guided in a particular area by a teacher sensitive to our status and progress—a mediator—we may appear to others to be unready. We can't perform because we haven't performed, and no one has taken us through the steps. This can be true of emotional issues, like learning to trust.

Those who are to instruct us tend to base their instruction on our present level of competence without reference to our potential. They may well underestimate the speed with which we *could* learn, given optimal help. In that case we stand a good chance of losing interest.

In fact, Csikszentmihalyi and his coworkers found that half of all gifted young people drop out of their area of special talent. They lose interest because the instruction is either dull or the classroom setting provokes anxiety rather than excitement.

Think about it: *half* drop out. If these figures can be generalized at all, the loss to society is incalculable. If the formally identified gifted individuals abandon their specialties, if they find little support for their gifts, little wonder an entire society complains of a diminishing quality of life.

The Self-Defined Challenge

As Antoine de Saint-Exupéry lamented, "too many are unawakened." Our sleepwalking is the source of our collective misery. We have been asleep to our subtler conflicts, our deep impasses, and our latent gifts. But having glimpsed the range of our nonconscious knowing, our rich "secret lives," we can hardly be content to go back to sleep.

Knowing that interest and intention are the movers and shakers of our very neurons, our next step is to undertake our own training.

There is a Sanskrit saying: *Gate, gate, paragate, parasamgate. Bodhi sava.* Translation: "Gone, gone, gone beyond, gone beyond the beyond. Hail the goer." Out of sheer necessity, the learner has gone beyond.

The abused child matures to become a compassionate psychotherapist. The paralyzed boy slowly and painfully types the words that will achieve literary acclaim. In an effort to appear normal, the one-armed girl learns to skate, then to perform gymnastics, and places second in a national competition. The young physicist, crippled and rendered almost mute by a degenerative disease, dazzles the world with his theories. The prince tries to escape from the straitjacket of his royal station to work for what he sees as the common good.

A self-defined challenge is an irresistible teacher.

Emotionally we're challenged either by the need or by the opportunity to overcome habitual behavior, such as criticizing, complaining, overreacting to criticism. We can also choose how we handle grief, disappointment, loss, frustration, boredom, loneliness, and the need to admit that we were wrong.

Intellectually we're challenged by new ideas and the need to revise old ones. We can improve the way we strategize, the way we design our personal experiments and educate ourselves. If we're quick, we're challenged to learn patience; if we are easily distracted, we are challenged to learn focus; if we tend to become dogmatic, we are challenged to listen to new ideas.

Physically we're challenged by toxins in the environment. We are challenged to improve our diet and adopt healthy new habits to increase energy.

Professionally we have to keep up with ideas and information, to maintain our standards and our enthusiasm, to cope with successes and setbacks, to know "when to hold and when to fold."

Spiritually we're challenged to live our values, to renew our faith, to love the unlovable and to forgive the unforgivable.

Socially we are challenged by the expectations of others. We're challenged by our relationships, by being labeled, and by the need to see past labels. We're challenged to know when to trust and when to say no.

Culturally and historically we're all challenged to learn the lessons of our group and to transcend our cultural limits. We are beset by problems for which there are no precedents. Above all we're challenged to reverse the classic pattern of history whereby high civilizations somehow lose their gifts and go into slow, pitiable decline.

In other words, we can deny the facts of this age or we can graciously accept a world in which change is the norm. Equipped as we are with self-transforming brains, we can all become successful athletes in life. Challenges and crises are the allies of intelligence.

6 CHOOSING TO BE INTELLIGENT

The Hunter-Gatherer and the Scout

To see clearly is poetry, prophecy and religion all in one.

—John Ruskin

I want to make the hidden obvious.

—Virginia Satir

The fact that challenge awakens and organizes our brains demands a new way of looking at intelligence. Conventional definitions are inadequate.

Some of us feel best about ourselves when we have managed our time well, others when we have done something creative, and still others when we have served well. Furthermore, our mental acuity varies from one day to the next, even from hour to hour. We can be shocked into or out of our wits.

If we're sick with the flu or a cold we are less alert, less able to think than usual. In other words, sometimes we are fully "intelligencing," and other times we are operating at less than our capacity.

The ups and downs of our self-esteem may be tied to how smart we feel at a given moment. Most of us would prefer that others doubted our motives rather than our intelligence. The nature and origin of intelligence has been a more delicate conversational subject than politics, sex, or religion.

Intelligent—For What?

Let's face it. Every ability, if used improperly—at the wrong time, in the wrong place, or at the wrong intensity—can be counterproductive. If otherwise talented people have a deficient sense of timing or if they are emotionally insensitive, we can see why they would not be living up to their potential.

Intelligence is like a Swiss army knife. It has many tools and components, and some of them are double-edged. By relying so heavily on tests we emphasize immediate performance as opposed to depth of understanding. It becomes more important to look smart than to *be* smart.

Which brings us to the question of purpose—the uses of intelligence. Intelligence cannot be isolated as a trait because it is context dependent. It has to be seen in relation to a given situation. When a manager remarked to Peter Drucker that he was looking for "a good man," the great management theorist asked, "Good for what?"

Psychologist Howard Gardner proposes the idea of multiple intelligences rather than intelligence. He identifies seven categories: linguistic, mathematical-logical, musical, spatial, bodily-kinesthetic, interpersonal (social), and intrapersonal (self-understanding).

Specific abilities come into play for sheer maintenance. Our basic survival intelligence makes sure that we don't run out of gasoline on a lonely road and that we take care of our obvious health needs. Certain creative skills, like the ability to visualize the steps to a project or product, also require what we might call compassionate skills—the ability to communicate and to inspire cooperation. Then there are specific facets of intelligence like craftsmanship or farming or juggling.

If we reexamine our notion of what it means to be smart, we have to take into account our ability to enjoy life. How intelligent can we be if our lives aren't working? And since life is always presenting fresh challenges, our definition of intelligence has to include the ability to change ourselves and to change our world. We need to know what the world requires of us, our own needs and goals, and how to set about meeting these requirements.

This suggests a whole arena of specific intelligences for life management: the ability to achieve liberating insights, to sharpen our awareness, to motivate ourselves, and to recover from setbacks. We can think of ourselves as behaving intelligently if we can ensure our survival, clarify our thoughts, freshen our senses, and keep our hearts and minds open. We need to recognize patterns, and sudden breaks from patterns. And we need to know when to rest, when to give up, and when to hang on by our fingernails.

Intelligence and Our Values

Even though we acknowledge that intelligence has many facets, we still value certain types more than others. Intelligence is often in the eye (or the mind) of the beholder.

And in the situation. Sometimes we need the counsel of a sensitive friend, sometimes we need business advice, sometimes we crave the company of someone with a quick humor. In the midst of a natural disaster the skills of a doctor might be more to the point.

To the point . . . that's the real issue. We are back to the issue of context: time and place. This is the aspect of intelligence we might call meaning or relevance. At such times our abilities do not exist in splendid isolation but rather join in a meaningful task.

For purposes of this journey, the highest measure of intelligence is the ability to do the right thing at the right time—to be appropriate. If ever we needed "genius in its working clothes" it's now. We don't wish to be overly mental in a situation of the heart, for example, or explode with creative ideas while balancing the checkbook.

Intelligence once meant to gather or select. Perhaps our forebears considered those people intelligent who (1) gathered or connected information and (2) selected wisely. In his long-range study of self-actualizers, Abraham Maslow observed that such people were "good choosers." They tended to make healthy choices in their work, their friends, even their marriage partners.

It is as if the various abilities were horses suitable for specific tasks—for racing, slow steady work, or intermediate distances. Intelligence is our stable of options.

Tensegrity and Intelligence

Tension, the pull between opposites, is an important part of our working intelligence. Thomas Kuhn, the philosopher of science who introduced the concept of paradigm shifts in science, spoke of "essential tension" in the creative process. The role of tension can best be seen in a metaphor: the "tensegrity structures" designed by Buckminster Fuller.

Their structural integrity is based on tension. Its structural strength, even greater than that of the geodesic dome, is due to its ability to absorb stress because of an inherent balance of distributed tension.

If we think of intelligence as a kind of fluid structure, we can see the value of abilities that might seem to be opposing: foresight and spontaneity, for instance, or conservation and innovation. As we develop a sense of timing, which might derive from observation and patience, we might also become more spontaneous. In other words, the tendency to make rapid decisions is compensated for by (1) a good memory for past mistakes or (2) a quick recovery.

We can learn a lot, incidentally, by noticing that we have underestimated another person's ability to turn a disaster around or to avert danger at the last moment. Sometimes what seemed a foredoomed marriage or calamitous undertaking turns out well. "Spoiled brats" sometimes turn out to be loving, accomplished people.

If we can identify in retrospect the qualities that we had not taken into account, we can begin to grasp some of the subtler or less visible aspects of intelligence. And we can learn from those occasions when we have overestimated the intelligence of certain individuals. What fooled us? Maybe we were unduly impressed by glibness, for example. As someone once said, "Beware of the articulate incompetent."

The house of our intelligence is constructed of so many cofactors, some of them evolutionary, that any of us would be presumptuous to think we know our own limits, let alone the limits of another.

Metastrategies

Intelligence has its tricks of the trade, principles that we might call "metastrategies." Discovering a single metastrategy can change the course of a life. In *The Potent Self* the great body therapist Moshe Feldenkrais describes some of the "great intelligences" who "recognized that their ability was mainly due to their method of using themselves."

Feldenkrais gave as an example philosopher Jean-Jacques Rousseau. Rousseau insisted on his lack of "natural" gifts and attributed all his achievements to his system of using himself, which took him many years to come by. He found his way, he says, by trying to read an author without approval or criticism—that is, without emotional bias. Feldenkrais wrote:

Rousseau's system was to learn to present the idea the author had in mind as clearly as possible, to the extent of being able to formulate it as well as the author would have liked. After prolonged apprenticeship in this skill, he found that his ability to formulate the ideas of other men clearly and vividly was increasing at a pace with his ability to think for himself. The methods he used before stumbling onto this idea never yielded anything comparable.

Rousseau was largely self-educated. It is easy to see how such a self-training strategy might lift a "normal" intelligence onto another plane entirely. His effort at a kind of intellectual empathy was a trick he had stumbled upon. One successful man says that when he was young he made up a "hit list" of people he wanted to meet, individuals whose work he admired. He made it his policy always to offer something in exchange, usually his labor or a gift. Somehow his offerings and his frank admiration did the trick. He was able to meet—and befriend—virtually everyone on his list.

Collective Intelligence

When a renaissance spirit or a collective breakthrough begins to revolutionize a group, city-state, or nation, popular intelligence also seems to be enhanced. We must remember that opera and the plays of Shakespeare were not just for the elite but for everyone.

The second half of the twentieth century is no island of high achievement. Our modern societies are not necessarily the apex of civilization, much as we would like to think so. In many places, on many occasions during humanity's odyssey on this planet, high thoughts and emotions have given birth to genius.

The idea of intelligence as an enterprise of government, as in espionage, had its origins in the determination of the Elizabethans to substitute science, information gathering, and communication for what they lacked in armed might or size. Every citizen who went abroad was expected to be alert and report on anything interesting.

The reputation of England's spy network was legendary. The queen of England, it is said, knew more about the Spanish Armada than the king of Spain.

In many ways, we are heirs to the idea that knowledge is power—that secrets, discoveries, data, and abstract concepts are more potent than armies or treasuries. Economic and cultural knowledge are more powerful than weapons.

The fruits of intelligence, spread throughout a land by improved crafts and practices, generate loyalty and cohesiveness among the people. It makes sense that modern society would be more inspired by a creativity race or an intelligence race than it is by an arms race. Intelligence can be cultivated—that is evident. The fact that most nations have not undertaken this cultivation implies only that there are stubborn myths or assumptions preventing us. Chief among these is the belief that intelligence is fixed. Also, education is usually reformed according to need rather than rethought according to opportunity.

Psychologists have pointed out that any test of intelligence should include a measure of the ability to pay attention and to use what one has learned, whereas traditional tests measure only the ability to store information. Attention, we might say, draws on our *radical common sense*.

If you continue to do what you've always done, you're going to get what you always got. Alas, or maybe Amen, it's that simple. Psychiatrist R. D. Laing expressed the same idea:

> The range of what we think and do
> is limited by what we fail to notice.
> And because we fail to notice
> that we fail to notice
> there is little we can do to change,
> until we notice how failing to notice
> shapes our thoughts and deeds.

Psychologist Jean Houston said of her travels to remote places:

> One of the things I like best is meeting so many people very much smarter than I. My experiences are very different from what I read about in the media. . . . The story I'm seeing is infinitely more complex.

As it becomes ever more evident that we haven't been using our common sense, it becomes clear that truer sensing might lead us out of our darkness. Soon we are looking differently, listening differently, tuning in.

Remember Colin Wilson's trick of "doubling attention." Good learners know how to interest themselves in information, how to make it vivid enough to remember. *At*tention sees, *re*tention remembers, *in*tention creates. We observe, we remember what we saw, and we choose to act.

John Steele, an archeologist and aroma therapist, points out that multisensory experience—common sensing, in effect—strengthens memory. Our ability to remember is a direct result of the quality of our original attention.

"I don't think I have a high I.Q.," novelist Edna O'Brien said, "but I have a pervasive intelligence. Everything interests me."

The Art of Noticing

Intelligence is less a matter of thinking cleverly than it is an exploration. Vision arises in part from the way we take in information. To carry forth the metaphor of a tribe migrating, let's picture the noticer as a scout. The scout is vigilant, open to all information.

Visionaries tend to notice more than most people or, at any rate, to be more interested in what they notice. The sense of having observed something significant that others have overlooked often motivates them in their projects or careers. Some people notice the need for a product or service. Others notice subtle attributes of people, including their own.

Paying attention, taking in more, reveals patterns of behavior in ourselves and others. Over time we can also see more readily how one event or idea is connected to another. We notice more frequently the sensations that are clues to our unconscious reactions—the primal feelings that arise continuously and spontaneously.

By maximizing our physical senses, we open the gateway to greater vision. The senses of the physical body train the senses of the mind's body. By observing as an artist or a detective, we more readily gain access to subtler seeing, to insight, and to the tacit knowing sometimes called intuition. By listening to the subtle sounds of the world around us and even the sounds inside our bodies we develop our "third ear." By observing the stream of our thoughts we come to that "consciousness without an object" that is the goal of many meditative practices. At such times whatever rises to attention does so effortlessly. Ideas just "occur" to us.

Noticing differs from anxious concentration. Most of us learned to tense up in order to pay attention. Certain vision problems, for instance, are attributable to a chronic tensing of the eye muscles in order to grasp information, especially in reading.

Visionary attention is a kind of receptivity. Maria Montessori called it "the absorbent mind." Individuals of genius, John Keats said, are characterized by "a receptivity to all experience: sorrow, joy, the commonplace, the heroic." Novelist Lawrence Durrell observed that patient, loving attention might help us see into the natural order of things.

True attention, writer Flora Courtois said, is rare and totally sacrificial. "It demands that we throw away everything we have been or hope to be, to face each moment naked of identity, open to whatever comes. . . ."

Nor is the potential for pain to be underestimated.

Now we come face to face with the radical fact that there is nothing, however dear, that cannot be taken from us from one moment to the next; nothing, however sinister or horrifying, from which we will be permitted to recoil or separate ourselves.

Careful observation, in fact, is central to seeing new solutions. If we see only that which we expect to, our expectations, not our eyes, are doing the looking.

Attention Is the First Teacher

This brings us to the heart of radical common sense: the power of attention. Attention to sensory input. Attention to feelings and sensations that are otherwise in the background. Attention to the fit of information and to the unspoken "field" of a person or situation. To our fragmentation. To changes of mood.

Attention is surely the first stratagem for learning; it's a key to how we know. Both William James and Colin Wilson have insisted that we can voluntarily light a fire under our attention.

The pertinent questions: How aware and awake do we choose to be? What unconscious elements are draining our attention? Are we eager or reluctant to uncover them? As someone said, "I don't know who discovered water, but you can be sure it wasn't a fish." Because we swim in the invisible medium of culture and history, our attention will never be filter free. Even so, if we can remove some of the less useful filters, we will pick up more information from the environment.

The word *attention* derives from the Latin *attendere*, "to stretch to." An interesting connection. We almost certainly underestimate the stretch required to be truly attentive.

Intelligence and Attention

A child's intelligence at age four can be predicted at four months by two factors. One is the quality of the mother-baby dialogue. The other is its eye movements. The attentive infant is always scanning the environment.

"Each of us literally chooses by his way of attending to things what sort of universe he shall appear to himself to inhabit," wrote William James in his landmark volume, *The Principles of Psychology*.

Firstborn and only children, as John Briggs points out, have more opportunity to focus. They have more undisturbed time than younger children do in a busy family, and so they develop a greater capacity to become absorbed.

This stronger "attention muscle" may help account for the disproportionate number of high achievers among firstborn and only children.

Attention is surprisingly powerful. In one experiment, paying attention to one's behavior was more effective in breaking habits than either punishment or reward. In another study, people were asked to pay attention to where their attention went. The effect was so extraordinary that some subjects thought they had been given a psychedelic substance.

One visionary, now a mother and a successful businesswoman, discovered that attention was the key to overcoming her illness. At twenty-two, confined to a wheelchair by multiple sclerosis, she signed up for a self-improvement seminar. "At some point during the weekend I realized that I had chosen relief from pain over being conscious." With that realization she gave up her analgesics and tried every treatment she heard of, so many she'll never know which resulted in her remarkable cure. But she is convinced that the pivotal point was her decision to feel, whatever the cost. "I had to wake up."

The ability to pay attention without prejudice, the watching of oneself, is what some spiritual technologies call "the Witness."

"What we are looking for," said Francis of Assisi, "is what is looking."

"The greatest thing a human soul ever does in this world is to see something and tell what it saw in a plain way," said John Ruskin, the nineteenth-century art critic and social prophet who opened the way for the Arts and Crafts Movement.

Physicist Richard Feynman said: "Our imagination is stretched to the utmost, not, as in fiction, to imagine things which are not really there, but just to comprehend those things which are there."

Meditation, alternative healing, introspective music, shamanic practices, dream journals, and the like help us pay attention. For most participants, the goal is to be more present. Those lucky enough to wake up from time to time are likely to aspire to even greater wakefulness. They are the most avid seekers of remedies for their sleep.

In learning to pay attention to our own attention, we become our own teachers. We begin to see how we draw our conclusions.

Training attention liberates the mind to do what it does best—receive. If we notice the role intuition plays in our solutions, we can direct our "figuring out" mind to serve our intuitive mind rather than overrule it.

A university president has described a coworker:

[He has] the classic trait of a seasoned bird-watcher or naturalist: the ability to sense—almost to see something ninety degrees to the right or left even while looking straight into someone's face. It's like having a third eye instinctively alert for the flutter of a wing or the swaying of a branch.

We cannot be attentive, obviously, if we are preoccupied with our thoughts. Frederick Leboyer, the French obstetrician whose gentle deliveries revolutionized childbirth practices in the 1970s, once remarked that he was leaving for India the following week. "What will you be doing there?" someone asked. Leboyer replied, "Nothing . . . very carefully."

Receptivity requires that we inhibit activity in the brain's occipital region, in the back of the head. In other words, a gate can be dropped, closing off our usual mental chatter so that subtler perceptions can rise to consciousness.

Rainer Maria Rilke said:

Whoever you are, some evening take a step out of your house, which you know so well . . . With your eyes slowly, slowly, lift one black tree up, so it stands against the sky: skinny, alone. With that you have made the world.

As our social challenges intensify, inventor Richard Lang said, "noticing will no longer be optional. Certain problems will force themselves on our attention. We notice that the summers are unusually sweltering or the winters more bitterly cold than we remember. We notice people with no place to live and garbage with no place to go. We notice that our leaders sometimes show up from unexpected places. We notice the effects of our not having noticed earlier.

"We notice noticing. And we may finally notice where we are as a society, in preparation for future decades when we discover who, what, and why we are. . . ."

As we will see, there is more to noticing than meets the eye.

7
TUNING IN TO THE FIELD
The Dowser

Sleeping or waking, we hear not the airy footsteps
of the strange things that almost happen.

—NATHANIEL HAWTHORNE

If facts are the seeds that later produce knowledge and wisdom,
then the emotions and the impressions of the senses are
the fertile soil in which the seeds must grow.

—RACHEL CARSON

On our journey to a new understanding the quest necessarily leads us through the shadowy domain of feelings and perceptions for which there is very little language. Recall Tom Paine's statement: "Our style and manner of thinking have undergone a revolution. We see with other eyes; we hear with other ears; and we think with other thoughts than those we formerly used."

Can we use our present eyes and ears to find these "other" modes of sensing?

Most creatures seem to have some kind of guidance system, such as ultrasensitive hearing and smell, whiskers, antlers, biological sonar, and antennae. In a way it would seem unreasonable if human beings were *not* equipped with an array of subtle senses similar to those of dolphins, bats, salmon, and our domestic pets. In fact, we do have such sensitivities, but for a variety of reasons most of us pay scant attention to them.

Many behaviors are associated with bonding between mothers and infants. A very young baby can distinguish the voice of its mother from other female voices and can even discern the scent of its own mother's milk. Yet researchers observing mothers playing with their infants found that only one-third out of a hundred were attentive to their babies' emotional signals.

One-third of the mothers could learn to recognize the infant's effort to communicate once it was pointed out to them. And one-third were completely unable to detect emotional signals from their children.

Philosopher E. H. Gutkind maintained that only by rediscovering the life instincts could humanity survive self-destruction. He said that in the highest type of activity, energy radiates "as from the sun itself." Henry Miller saw in Gutkind's message the possibility of "a spiritual revolution which would lead right into the midst of the new time . . . a spiritual climate in which the body will no longer be denied."

In this instance Miller was not championing sexual freedom, the cause for which he is best remembered. Rather, he was talking about our general tendency to postpone life—what he called "the refusal to overflow."

Just as creative individuals tend to be unusually observant of their surroundings, many are equally alert to their inner life—twinges, inner dialogue, gut feelings, tones, surges of energy. The hairs on their neck may stand on end. Through these inner sensations, they seem to pick up unspoken communications from others in the environment, seeing past social facade. "Artists," Ezra Pound once said, "are the antennae of the world."

As we heighten our attention in general, we perceive more "out there." Gradually we may also become aware of other sensations. For example, human beings have a homing sense not unlike that of pigeons. Interestingly, this sensitivity seems to be more pronounced when there is no visual input. In one experiment people were blindfolded, then taken on circuitous routes to distant places. Even when taken to an island and spun around, they could point toward home. When the blindfolds were removed, their accuracy diminished. A magnetic bar placed on their foreheads eliminated the ability. Material in our brains links us to Earth's natural field.

The Body Electric

In laboratory settings people routinely detect faint changes in the gravitational field. Some people are even "allergic" to electricity. They become confused, or their moods change. They may weep or complain of physical pain when they are around ordinary electrical fields. Such people are affected by common electronic devices like audio and video recorders, computers, household appliances, navigational aids, computerized fuel injection systems in cars, and even electronic watches. In an allergic state, they actually emit measurable levels of electromagnetic radiation, enough to play havoc with electronic equipment.

Some aspect of the brain is always scanning the environment even if we are asleep or lost in thought. Specific brainwave changes in the laboratory are evidence that even in deep sleep people react when their name is spoken.

Like the cells of our body, we can sense each other. Bonds of family, affection, and even proximity produce physical effects. For instance, when a man and a woman live together, the male partner gradually falls into temperature rhythms that correspond to his partner's ovarian cycle. The synchrony disappears if she begins taking a contraceptive. Female friends living together in a household or dormitory wing tend to have simultaneous menstrual cycles. Researchers in Mexico placed pairs of human subjects in a shielded environment, then instructed them to "tune into" each other. The pairs generated remarkably similar EEG patterns.

We can learn to detect these faint kinesthetic signals just as we might notice a color or a noise.

Listening to the Field

It's curious, in a way, that the research on nonverbal communication attracts attention. After all, we have been addressing each other nonverbally all along.

Sometimes the metacommunication overwhelms language itself. As the saying goes, "What you are speaks so loudly I can't hear what you say." We communicate by our apparel, movements, silences, posture, tones, the lightness or heaviness of our words and our bearing. Our presence is the medium and the message.

The mechanical smile, the taut shoulder. "It wasn't what you said, it was how you said it."

We have been speaking and listening on multiple levels. But because we don't usually acknowledge the field, the meta-communication, we are frustrated.

Humanity has always been aware of the field. Art historian Jose Arguelles calls it the *salsa de vida*, the dance between and among living organisms. When athletes say, "I lost it," they aren't talking about losing the game, or the race, per se. They lost *it*—their link to the present moment, their connection to the field.

At its most blatant, a connection to the field translates into star quality, charisma, the little light that shines briefly through all of us from time to time and pours from some people like a Vesuvian fountain.

Feeling Tones, the Primal Palette

Many people deliberately tune into and use felt information. Feeling, as we use the term, is sensibility, the ability to perceive sensations, not emotion per se (as in "getting in touch with your feelings").

A feeling can lead to an emotion, an idea, or an action. And sometimes it does all three. Felt information is not black-and-white. It is subtle, literally, in the word's original meaning, "finely woven." We have to attend to it deliberately because it won't force itself upon us. The same intentionality that goes into listening like a cat or watching like a hawk is required if we want to develop inner sensibility.

It makes sense that tuning into this information is a means for fine-tuning our intelligence. In recent years, researchers from many disciplines have converged on the possibility that feeling is the organizer of thought.

The regions of the brain involved in feeling are crucial to cognitive knowing. The old emotional brain (limbic system), linked more to the right hemisphere than the left, is vital to our functional intelligence.

In a model proposed by psychiatrist William Gray and systems theorist Paul LaViolette, feelings are combined and recombined like colors on a palette to give form to our concepts. In other words, we recall what we know because of the subtle feelings associated with it. These feelings are like highlighter pens, marking events as more or less relevant.

A concept like "right angle," for instance, has a felt or body sense as well as a visual sense. Having once seen a circular staircase might later help us to encode integral calculus.

When we access a memory we trigger a kind of body image. This is why it's so difficult to learn something for which we "have no feeling." And it begins to explain why schooling is so inefficient and why students complain of boredom. If teaching fails to stimulate the feeling center, our brains aren't fully engaged. The material has no emotional hook. Mere memorization is harder to recall and use. Indeed, good learners seem to create interest through their own sense of purpose.

Memory, in this model, is a chain of nuances. Feeling tones glue our experiences together. Creative scientists have described the importance of a kinesthetic sense—something feels wrong or suddenly fits.

William Gray was led to this model by Einstein's repeated statement that ideas came to him first in the form of vague and diffuse bodily sensations that gradually refined themselves into reproducible feeling tones. One of these was the sense that the universe is somehow a continuum. Novelist Virginia Woolf was preoccupied with waveforms, which she traced to her earliest memory of infancy. Science historian Gerald Holton calls felt images "themata." Each of us is moved by early experiences.

Tuning Out

If feelings are invaluable to problem-solving, why this common tendency to overrule or disregard them? What keeps this privileged information out of our conscious range?

First of all, there is our basic training in denial. When we were small we learned to control the signals from our bladder, we learned that it is sometimes mannerly to say no to food when we are hungry or yes when we are not. We learned to control our tears and muffle our amusement, to sit still, and to manage our sexual impulses.

Impulse control is essential to social functioning, but it need not inhibit our feeling life. Admitting our feelings into awareness is itself an act, an inner gesture. As these feelings are illuminated by attention, they can be incorporated into our conscious agenda. As we become ever more adept at taking in our feelings, they tend to flow through us rather than drown us.

Another barrier is our lack of interior "community." We tend to relate to our subselves separately.

Most of the time we address our feelings as they chance to arise, giving precedence to the loudest ones. We may listen to the harping, intellectual self, or the easily distracted self, or some nagging physical symptom like a tired back. We seldom step back to take in the entire spectrum of our feelings, to see which subselves might be missing.

Having been trained to ignore our feelings in social situations, and being a clever species, we commonly use dissociative skills against discomfort or pain. If "I" feel troubled, "I" can think about something else. What this means is that the troubled "I" steps aside. It doesn't go away.

We can check out the built-in pain suppression mechanism by performing a little experiment the next time we're injured—a twisted ankle, a burn, a bumped shin. The pain is almost instantaneous, of course, then it dulls a bit. After a moment, if we deliberately invite it to expand to its full limits, its natural boundary, we allow it to change.

The pain will probably intensify at that moment, at least for a time; if we consciously remain open to it, it will usually diminish or even cease abruptly. We may be gratified to find that our injury is less damaging than we might have expected. The bruise may be smaller than usual, the cut or burn less swollen.

When we are injured, the body tends to rush in with emergency procedures triggered, in part, by our anxiety—the sight of blood, the re-experiencing of past injuries, maybe the fear that we'll lose productive time. Worrisome possibilities flash before us. As physician Lewis Thomas once said of the body's tendency to overreact to most viruses, the "cure" is more traumatic than the original complaint. The Pentagon of our defense mechanisms rushes in with troops and materiél.

The fact that we are able to enlarge the pain after the initial trauma means that some innate pain-suppression mechanism had gone to work almost immediately. Our ability to deepen the pain after an initial trauma means that we were keeping that pain out of awareness—a phenomenon called "battlefield anesthesia." Its adaptive value is obvious. And the fact that deliberately experiencing the pain often brings about its cessation is evidence that the body has other tricks up its sleeve. A higher level of pain engages certain long neurons capable of bringing relief.

Mental and Emotional Discomfort

Most of the time our discomfort stems from mental and emotional stressors. We are likelier to have nightmares about public humiliation than about physical danger. Still, the mechanisms are analogous.

We have a tendency to oversimplify. Reluctant to deal with contradictions in our philosophy, say, we muffle spontaneous feelings that run counter to our stereotypes. Complexity is the natural enemy of our comfort. Having "made up our minds" about certain things (God, sex, political issues, people) we don't want to go to the trouble of remaking them.

Psychologist Ernest Becker said:

> Each person literally closes off his world, fences himself around, in the very process of his own growth and organization. In order to have some kind of centered control over his acts, the individual sets limits on his range of action, on the spectrum of his thought and feeling: It must all be marshaled and harbored within control.

Positive feelings, of course, tend to open us up to new people and ideas. The open feeling we call love, or even mild attraction, dissolves these barriers. As youngsters we're less guarded in our enthusiasms, quicker to open our hearts to people and ideas.

Name Your Filter

We all have mood swings, alternating between excitement and despair. We may "veg out," become a "couch potato." The "normal" daytime sleepiness of adults reported by researchers may be a defense against feeling.

We may disconnect from our feelings altogether—a condition called alexithymia. Neuroscientists suggest that many of us have effectively split our brains without benefit of surgery. We have walled off feeling from verbal expression.

High blood pressure can be a defense against feeling. As our blood pressure rises, we become physically less sensitive. Interestingly, this rise in blood pressure is hierarchical; those lower on the socioeconomic totem pole tend to have the greater blood elevation when listening. People typically show a greater elevation when their blood pressure is taken by a doctor than when it is taken by a nurse or technician.

One laboratory experiment revealed a great deal about the mechanism. Subjects were (falsely) led to believe that they would experience a shock at some point during the single experimental session. Throughout the session, experimenters measured the subjects' muscle tension and heart rate. Afterward, participants were asked to choose one of two statements as the more descriptive of their state during the session.

The subjects split almost evenly into two groups. The avoiders described themselves as passive. Feeling confined and restricted, they had tried to, as one put it: "escape the . . . situation by focusing my attention on nonstressful targets. I want to keep [the shock] away as long as possible. I wished to avoid thinking about the stressor."

The confronters, on the other hand, tended to think they could do something about the stressful situation, if only to prepare for it. They took into account an ever greater number of probabilities. They looked around the laboratory. They sought information that might prepare them for the shock.

The physical responses of the two groups? The avoiders showed an elevated blood pressure. The confronters' trapezius muscles tensed up in anticipation of the shock that never came, a healthier response.

What a predicament. We've reduced the input of our feelings because they hurt too much. Yet we can't function well without them, so now we're in chronic discomfort.

Such is the cost of unconsciousness, of keeping a roof over our unwanted data. Do we dare reclaim this territory?

Social Distractions as Anesthesia

Sensational news and entertainment distract us from the sensations closer to home. At the same time, the externalized drama—wars, victories, mythic romances, and scandals—can make our own hopes and fears seem petty by comparison. Even the political rhetoric can serve as a distraction from troubling personal issues.

One young man remarked that he keeps the radio on at all times "so I don't have to listen to my thoughts." Many people report a kind of background dread, the feeling that even though everything is all right now, trouble is just around the corner. Others are afraid that they will be flooded with memories of past and present sins and mistakes.

Ironic, isn't it, how the outer world distracts us from the murky inner world, yet it is precisely the inner world that might furnish us answers to our outer crises. It is the inner scriptwriter, with meaning and metaphors uniquely our own, who can inspire, enrich, and heal us far more than any outer drama.

Our inner needs may be waylaid, but they do not go away. Maybe they translate into physical symptoms. Or maybe they mutate into unrealistic ambitions or causes. At least now, if we feel unhappy, it's because something out there is thwarting us. Little wonder that public life so often degenerates into a shouting match. Inflammatory charges by opposing groups, movie violence, televised conflict—these feed and are fed by our inward apprehension.

Over time, we can freeze our feeling life into righteous, rigid personal codes. "I never drink coffee." "I can't live without my coffee." "I never vote." "I always obey the law." "I hate people like that." Behavioral and emotional rigidity keeps us from seeing what's before us.

We all shy away from changing our minds.

The Dangers of Anesthesia

Those who would mastermind the society and manipulate us are well aware of the unspoken communication. Marketers, advertisers, performers, speech writers, and product designers profit from our unacknowledged needs and desires.

The voice-over in the commercial sounds like a favorite uncle. Fast-food restaurants surround us with red and yellow and play loud fast music to accelerate our eating. Public speakers use the rhythm of their rhetoric to lull us into a hypnotic trance.

The brain is a guessing instrument. It was born to be tricked. If we don't discover what fools us and how, we will be pawns of those who have made the "field" their field. We need to be able to read people—what they mean, not what they say—a survival skill more fundamental than the reading of words. Having consigned our feelings to Hallmark, we've lost touch with our gut-knowing and become the victims of our own façade.

We may finally ask, "Will the real me please stand up?"

8 REKINDLING THE FLAMES OF INTUITION

The Firemaker

Set yourself on fire, and people will come from miles around to see you burn.

—UNKNOWN

You have to leave the city of your comfort and go into the wilderness of your intuition. What you'll discover will be wonderful. What you'll discover is yourself.

—ALAN ALDA

Lightning, meteorites, volcanoes—such natural phenomena gave our ancestors their first experience of fire. We can only imagine how awesome flames were to their curious eyes, how beautiful, mysterious, and intimidating. We have to admire their efforts to conjure up this blazing deity with sticks and flint.

According to Greek legend, fire was given to humankind by the god Prometheus, whose unilateral decision angered the other Olympians. Polynesians in the Cook Islands maintain that the god Maui went to hell and back to retrieve the flaming gift. A Native American myth credits the buffalo. As the herd ran at night their hooves struck against the rocks causing sparks that set the brush ablaze.

By making it possible to live in colder regions, firemaking inspired people to migrate, thus shifting the centers of civilization. Other than language and agriculture, no development has more significantly shaped our social evolution than the ability to make fire.

A bolt of lightning is one thing, and the ability to light your own fire is quite another. Just as our ancestors could move about more freely with their blazing technology, we can more freely innovate and solve problems by getting more in touch with our intuition.

Kindling Sensations

William Gray's proposal that cognition itself is organized by feelings was verified, in part, by psychologist Eugene Gendlin of the University of Chicago. Gendlin developed a technique called "focusing," in which attention to a "felt sense" produces spontaneous insights.

The universe of feelings seems to have a profound logic all its own. "The heart has its reasons," Blaise Pascal wrote, "that reason knows not of." Great poets and scientists have praised the role of vague feelings in alerting the muse.

If our goal is to become more visionary we would be foolish not to pay more attention to subtle sensations. Feelings are the bridge between mind and matter. They are the lingua franca, the universal language between our intellect and our biocomputers. They describe associations and possibilities, offering clues for vigilance or attraction.

The word *intuition* comes from the Latin *intuere*, to know instinctively. Occasionally we'll hear someone say that their intuition didn't "prove out." But an intuition is correct by definition. If an occasional hunch doesn't hit, either it was misinterpreted or wrongly executed. We might get a strong signal that requires timing and strategy. The first flush of an intuitive knowing is an impetus, not a permanent blueprint. Sometimes we follow inner guidance that leads us into a painful situation. It may be that our higher intelligence sets us up for hard but necessary lessons.

There are also the little hunches that get us through the week. We say, "I have a feeling," or "It occurs to me . . ." In the ebb and flow, intuition sometimes flourishes like a gracious servant. It can also jump in like an older brother when we're tossed about by the rapids.

At times intuition seems fickle. This patron saint of pilgrims and parents, the finder of lost things, sometimes disappears without a trace. Not only do we not know who's calling when the phone rings, we don't know what to say when we answer. By strange coincidence we run into people we don't want to see.

Synchronicity turns on us, or so it seems.

When the feeling tone of our lives goes from promising to dire, and it looks like nothing will ever go right again, it's time for a little introspection.

Sometimes we're too anxious. During a crisis when we most need our intuition, our inner dialogue may be so shrill it drowns out the subtle whispers. Sometimes signals flow less freely because we're too hot or too cold or the barometric pressure is high. The distress of others also affects us.

Instinctively "Into It"

People commonly use the terms *intuition* and *instinct* interchangeably. An instinct is sudden, a reflex. We blink to protect our eyes. We have parental instincts, sexual instincts, feeding instincts. We instinctively crave certain foods.

Instinct and intuition both take advantage of subliminal perception. A part of us responds to sounds too low to cross the auditory threshold and images too fleeting to be described.

In sleep our brainwaves alter when our name is spoken. Comatose people may show an EEG response to questions asked.

But then much of our straightforward "normal" perception also remains a mystery. Radical common sense tells us to follow our hunches and see what happens. Emerson once said:

All our progress is an unfolding, like the vegetable bud. You have first an instinct—then an opinion—then a knowledge, as the plant has a root, bud and fruit . . . trust the instinct to the end, though you can render no reason. It is vain to hurry it. By trusting it to the end it shall open into truth and you shall know why you believe.

Operating without intuition is like hiking in the wilderness without reference to the sun. Intuition is an "inexplicable and sometimes ineffable sense of knowing that rises spontaneously into awareness, usually without forethought" (*Webster's Collegiate Dictionary*). Intuition can occur through a variety of modes—energy stirring in a bodily region, an auditory tone, an unspoken command, a compulsion to move or act. A sudden strike like "a bolt out of the blue."

We speak also of "trained" intuition. There's the investor's "Midas touch" and the athlete's "zone" when time stands still for the perfect play. "Woman's intuition" prompts a mother to catch a toddler tumbling off a chair. Professional bomb disarmers say they "see" the layout of a device before reaching in to disable it.

The Cult of Numbers doesn't intimidate the Firemaker, whose intuitive mind crunches numbers in its sleep. The Firemaker discerns subtle differences in color, texture, pitch, and qualities of taste. Two people meet at a place that neither expects to be. And suddenly a vision with the chance of "a snowball in hell" is a done deal.

We have to distract the linear mind to let full knowledge through, but it gets easier over time as we gather our bag of tricks.

The Body Instrument

By the time we're adults most of us have done a fair job of subordinating our bodies to the rulership of our heads. We block unwanted pain and discomfort. That is the undoing of our intuition, which speaks as much through sensation as thought.

Intuition and feeling can be thought of as kindred processes, sometimes one and the same.

Without intuition our visions aren't likely to get beyond early stages. Intuition rings a bell when a vision is worth pursuing. If we take on challenges it becomes a guide, lighting our way, evaluating circumstances, nudging us toward opportunities and useful allies. Our first task: the reunion of our various disembodied parts—brains, minds, hearts, and wills. We have to remember that which was dismembered in the name of numbness—feelings, emotion, sensation, intuition.

Intuitive signals alert us to knowledge regarding everyday events and decisions. To rekindle intuition we have to notice even the faintest sensations.

Unacknowledged feelings are like unread correspondence from a very real part of ourselves. If we ignore them they don't go away. They pile up like unpaid bills.

Freud called dreams the royal road to the unconscious. *Radical common sense is the royal road to intuition.*

By sitting quietly with an affect like fear or excitement we locate a specific body region where it originates. Simple attention often produces a radical shift.

By learning to track signals, we become the scouts of our inner terrain, picking up ever more subtle sensations. The intuitive sense draws from all our faculties, including the neglected kinesthetic sense.

Feelings may stir for days before a major revelation. It's as if on some level the old way of thinking already gave way, and a new mind is being built in the body. "Things are coming together," we say, but we'd be hard put to explain what we mean.

In Dante's *Divine Comedy*, Virgil, who symbolizes reason, cannot accompany the hero into Paradise. Before leaving Purgatory, Dante has a frightening dream. A distorted woman casts a spell on him and imprisons him in libido. Virgil directs his attention to a woman "holy and alert"—Beatrice, who breaks the spell with her voice.

If a man is not awake to the Beatrice within—what Jung calls the anima—the rejected feminine or receptive self distorts into the Siren, who promises cheap pleasure and power.

Blaise Pascal insisted that there is a feeling-based logos rooted in the body.

"Do you love by reason?"

Pascal argued for a return to a body-felt dialogue—the expression of feelings. Thinking alone will never cure what ails us. "We prove by logic," Henri Poincaré said, "but we discover by intuition."

Philip Goldberg points out that people ignore a lot of pertinent information by demanding reasons. "They seldom say, 'Give me one good feeling why you think John is wrong.'"

Quantum physicist David Bohm referred to thought as "the devil that got us into this mess." Architect Frank Lloyd Wright observed that the truth is more important than facts.

A Burning Sense

Without the support of intuition we would be slow to realize our visions. Intuition is a kind of shorthand of the mind, a form of thought closer to tuning in than to thinking. Emerson liked to speak of it as "inner-tuition," the counterpart of instruction from the outer world.

Intuition seems to derive in part from curiosity, the wonder we experience in subtle sensations and signals. This drives people to keep searching for fresh concepts rather than settling for "the answer." Fruitful intuition, Jerome Bruner said, carries with it a perpetual sense of incompleteness, a feeling that there is yet more to be known or done. Part of the visionary experience is the impression that life holds endless revelations.

Because intuition takes leaps like a dream or a wild animal we assume it cannot be harnessed. Bruner's view is that intuition should be "backstopped and disciplined" by rigorous ways of asking and solving problems. By noticing which hunches prove out, and which do not, we can read signals more accurately in the future.

We develop an intuitive language for this unknowing knowing.

Yet intuition is often rigorous itself, Bruner points out. For example, much of our mathematics was built on "Euler's Proofs," an intuitive set of concepts not proven for almost a century after they came into use. Bruner maintains that as children we knew a great deal more than we could prove, or even verbalize.

It's commonplace for practitioners of creative vision to be inarticulate about their insights. Most languages have relatively few words to describe inner events. Those foolhardy enough to try to explain their process are sometimes accused of "confabulating," or lying, by the very ones who ask.

Children quit talking about their inner lives early on. Only a rare family or classroom encourages conversation about such intangibles. Yet nearly everyone has had an experience of sudden, uncanny knowing. Through computations too complex to track, we "know" information before it occurs or before we are told.

Spontaneous Combustion

Deliberately increasing one's awareness of felt information can serve as an organic therapy. In *A Life of One's Own*, Joanna Field recounted a three-year odyssey when she determined to keep a diary of events that triggered a state of deep happiness.

> I had thought I was happy when I was having what was generally considered "a good time." But when I began to try and balance up each day's happiness, I had found that there were certain moments which had a special quality of their own, a quality which seemed to be almost independent of what was going on around me, since they occurred sometimes on the most trivial occasions.

She realized that these were moments when she had chanced to stand aside and look at her experience, "wanting nothing and prepared for anything." Now she set out to discover what this ability to "look" depended on.

I had set out by using the scientific method of observation, to find out what made me happy, and then found that it had led me beyond the range of science. For in observing what made me happy I had found something which could not be communicated, something which was an essentially private affair.

She rediscovered a way of knowing she'd surrendered as a child.

Then I had found that there was an intuitive sense of how to live. For I had been forced to the conclusion that there was more in the mind than just reason and blind thinking, if you only knew how to look for it; the unconscious part of my mind seemed to be something definitely more than a storehouse for the confusions and shames I dared not face. For was there not also the wisdom which had been shaped by my body up through the years from a single cell?

Her exploration made her aware of the existence of something ("I can only call it a wisdom") that had been shaping her ends.

Field, whose real name was Marion Milner, later became a well-known therapist.

Testing the Flame

How do we develop accuracy in distinguishing wishful thoughts and impulses from genuine intuitions?

Many say their intuitions are not overlaid with emotion; they are straightforward, often suggesting actions they did not have in mind or even resisted. Quite a few say they postpone action to see if the signals persist. The kind of hunches that pan out typically keep recurring.

A book editor says that she feels informative sensations in her body, distinct from events in her head. A former high school principal speaks of a thickness and texture "different from the cotton-candy nature of wishes." A well-known therapist says she developed a "body knowing" that is "more tangible than thoughts. When things seem to come out of the blue they generally prove to be the right move."

A psychiatrist said that for him intuition is accompanied by a sense of joy and is more convincing than a thought. "It focuses on concrete outcomes."

A seminar leader previews the contemplated move and checks for sensations in his chest. "If it's only wishful thinking I generally feel a contraction around my heart."

Another psychiatrist, who writes on the uses of imagery, said he checks for depth of conviction. "Generally speaking, I can tell the difference between intuition and wishful thinking by noticing whether or not I have to talk myself or anyone else into the idea."

"An impulse feels like a physical and emotional push and pull," said one doctor. "Intuition comes with calm, mindful awareness. It's relaxing and exciting at the same time." A former law enforcer says intuition has a certain wholeness; complete in itself. A "loving creation" rather than a reaction to something.

A film executive says she establishes hard deadlines for carrying out the intuition by analyzing its viability and talking it over with others. An inventor-entrepreneur says he subjects intuitions to logical scrutiny and feedback from trusted friends. "If it feels real after that, it probably is."

A magazine publisher says he waits twenty-four hours before acting on an intuition, his strategy for combating a tendency toward impulsive behavior.

An artist stands on one leg and tries to maintain balance. "Usually I can do it," she remarked. "If not, I remain skeptical."

Intuition is something to continually test and refine. Using all of one's resources is a visionary tradition. Because intuition offers a more efficient route to a goal, the very creative tend to train their ability.

The Sacred Heart-Mind

A willingness to trust subtle information is a reliable predictor of personal success and achievement. Certain people are chosen as exemplars—individuals who have repeatedly followed their hunches and made them work.

Even people who virtually make their reputations on their prescience report that too often they overrule their gut feelings, inner voices, or visual premonitions. Even knowing the cost of not trusting their intuition, they forget to remember to check inner signals.

A passage from Christopher Fry's 1945 play, *A Sleep of Prisoners*, seems more apt than ever:

> The human heart can go to the lengths of God. Dark and cold we may be, but this is no winter now. The frozen misery of centuries breaks, cracks, begins to move. The thunder is the thunder of the floes, the thaw, the flood, the upstart Spring. Thank God our time is now when wrong comes up to meet us everywhere, never to leave us, till we take the longest stride of soul men ever took.

Return to the Sacred

As children we spun out imaginary scenarios. Sometimes the intensity of our vision exceeded that of the local reality. It was usually at that point that adults demanded we subdue our play. So we continue to be attracted to this mysterious realm, yet a little afraid.

The popular song, "Aquarius," spoke about a time of the mind's true liberation. Maybe that time is now. We could think about it for a while. We could investigate, or ask around.

On the other hand, we could check our intuition. After all, we have nothing to lose.

9

THE DRIVE TO DISCOVER

The Artist-Scientist

At times I see myself as an artist and a poet,
and science is my medium.

—JONAS SALK

If art is to nourish the roots of our culture, Society must set
the artist free to follow his vision wherever it takes him.

—JOHN F. KENNEDY

Art and science are not so much disciplines as ways of seeing. Both are methods of discovery. By considering how artists and scientists are alike and different we can better understand ourselves. Social historian Lewis Mumford said that the test of maturity for nations, as well as for individuals, "is not the increase of power but the increase of self-understanding, self-control, self-direction, and self-transcendence." In a mature society we ourselves are the chief work of art.

Scientific rigor empowers an artist, and an esthetic sense inspires the scientist. The word *art* derives from the Latin *ars*, "skill," and *science* from *scientia*, "knowledge." Science represents the gathering of knowledge. Art, going beyond the information given, creates something new. Science must be practiced artfully if it is to go beyond mere fact finding.

The academic standoff between art and science, made famous in C. P. Snow's essay on the "Two Cultures," is not so much a war of disciplines as a failure to see that good art and good science are old bedfellows.

In a broad sense, art is not a product but the original impulse to invent, improve, and envision. The brain's analytical left hemisphere and the whole-seeing right hemisphere work together in successful innovation. Neurologically speaking, each of us is an artist-scientist seeking answers and framing never-ending questions.

"Perhaps I should feel deeper inner contradictions," Miroslav Holub, a Czech scientist and poet, told a group of American scientists. "But I simply never closed the door after high school, when everybody switches from a biology class or a physics class into a literature class. It's just changing rooms, not minds or cultures."

It is surely not by chance that the Golden Age of Greek science coincided with the Golden Age of Greek literature and art. Art flourished during the Italian Renaissance when printing made scientific knowledge from many cultures widely available. The explosion of physics in Munich in the 1920s was attributed by Werner Heisenberg to the rich intermingling of artists and scientists.

The Jugular Question

How does an artist choose? A long-range study at the University of Chicago, initiated in the 1960s started with psychologist Jacob Getzels's hunch that the heart of creativity is not problem solving but problem *finding*—selecting a task.

Getzels and Mihaly Csikszentmihalyi decided to study the creative process in a specific area: fine art.

Thirty-one male students from the Art Institute of Chicago took part. Each chose from among twenty-seven objects to create a still life, then set to work. The artists were minutely observed and their drawings were photographed at various stages.

Later all the drawings were exhibited for review by artist-critics. Seven years later, only those whose work had been rated best were actually supporting themselves by their work. The others had dropped out or now worked at their art part-time.

Bear in mind that the aim of the experimenters was to understand the creative process in general. The experimenters wanted to know if the process of choosing affects success or failure. "I decided to go for the jugular question," Getzels put it.

Several significant differences between the better artists and their fellow students stand out:

Delay of closure: The successful artists handled more objects before starting to work. They took longer to begin, but their total time on the project was not greater. Typically they worked first at one corner of the paper, then another. "To an observer it seemed they were not getting anywhere," the researchers said. "Yet toward the end they pulled the various parts of the work together into an organized whole."

The artists themselves expressed surprise at the sudden emergence of the final form. Apparently, they had simply trusted their intuition. They were less likely than the other group to think that their pictures would be harmed by being changed.

Art as a quest: When the less successful artists in the study were asked why they pursued their art, they usually responded in terms of the product—a surprising effect, a blend of colors. The successful artists valued the process, the act of drawing. "It's a basic questioning. . . ." "I'm trying to discover what my intentions are." "I like to look at people once removed, to understand and enjoy them." Or: "I draw to understand myself," or death, or relationships.

For them art was an inquiry into the human condition. They were likelier than the other artists to choose human figures from among the twenty-seven objects.

Other differences: The successful artists were more passionate, more pragmatic and more distrustful of their own success, intent on not repeating themselves. They had better grades on their studio work than did the other artists but did less well academically. Noting that the successful artists didn't score particularly well on standard tests of esthetic judgment, the researchers pointed out that such tests are based on established values, whereas successful artists help create new appetites rather than satisfy familiar ones.

In short, the successful artists in the University of Chicago study were doers not scholars. And they were leery of getting caught up in a role or a style. Most said they had not been unusually talented as children, but compared to their peers they were given more parental support.

At what point does that encouragement translate into the ability to give courage to oneself?

The Reverent, Irreverent Scientist

In analyzing the lives of more than two thousand scientists, Dean Keith Simonton found that the highest achievers typically had parents who exposed them to a rich variety of experiences without imposing a rigid belief structure.

Also like the successful artists, the eminent scientists were reverent about the mysteries they probed but irreverent toward prevailing attitudes and beliefs. Successful scientists are those who can make "rich associations of ideas."

In a survey, eminent scientists tended to agree with the statement that too much training in a specific field can stifle students and convert them to a particular point of view. The person who set out to be an experimenter is now bent on proving something. When a scientist aligns with a "church" within a discipline, there will be few surprises—or discoveries.

We confuse the venerable idea of science with the modern invention of the scientific method. The scientific method, by and large, is a system for studying phenomena that are observable, repeatable, and predictable. It typically limits the kinds of questions that can be addressed. Because the method emphasizes objective data, scientists have to pretend that they are not excited—not subjective—about their work.

Although inspiration and serendipity have only recently been discussed publicly among scientists, the visionary scientists offer their brethren—and the rest of us—a model of radical common sense. Having observed that clues come unbidden, we can learn to listen before we leap to conclusions. T. H. Huxley urged scientists to "sit before each fact like a little child."

James Olds, already an eminent neuroscientist, was curious about why one laboratory rat kept returning to the electric grid voluntarily to receive a shock. He saw that an electrode had been placed in the wrong region of the rat's brain. Further experiments led to Olds's discovery of the brain's pleasure centers.

The model scientist-artist, of course, is the person who takes theory into the realm of product. "To be a good inventor," said Stanford Ovshinsky, who pioneered the use of amorphous crystalline material in semiconductors, "you have to have a physical intuition, a feel I call perfect pitch."

An inventor's intuition is "a different kind of logic," Ovshinsky said. The idea itself emerges from a kind of metalogic "with many parallel paths operating simultaneously, perhaps subconsciously, based on a lot of seemingly unrelated information." Indeed, studies showed that breakthrough scientists think more like artists than like other scientists.

Scientist as Artist

"Imagination," Einstein said unequivocally, "is more important than knowledge."

More recently biochemist Robert Root-Bernstein proposed that training in the arts is almost a prerequisite for a certain level of high achievement in science. A study of one hundred fifty outstanding scientists revealed that most were involved in art, music, or literature. These pursuits presumably trained their ability to detect patterns and breaks in pattern.

J. H. van't Hoff studied two hundred scientists who were also artists. Of all the traits a scientist can have, van't Hoff concluded, imagination is the most crucial.

Galileo and Pasteur were poets, Kepler a musician and an artist. Root-Bernstein names many twentieth-century scientists with artistic leanings, including physicists Murray Gell-Mann, a poet, and Max Planck, a musician. Werner Heisenberg speculated that "the world of poetry has been familiar to all really great scientists."

Lev Vygotsky, the gifted and influential Russian psychologist, started as a poet and literary critic. His deep love of language led him to many of his important discoveries, for example, what he called "inner speech." Neuroscientist Candace Pert, codiscoverer of the opiate receptors, switched her college major from English literature to chemistry after receiving what seemed to her an unfair grade on an essay. ("I decided to go into a field where there was some objective method of judging whether or not your intuitions were right.") William James, the fountainhead of modern psychology, studied art seriously as a teenager. Einstein played the piano as well as the violin, and would run through arpeggios whenever he was at an impasse in his scientific thinking. Ilya Prigogine, Nobel laureate chemist, was a concert pianist in his youth.

Several of the framers of the American republic pursued both scientific and artistic interests. Benjamin Franklin's first publication was a successful poem, and he vigorously pursued literary excellence. As a scientist he became world-famous for his discoveries about electricity, weather, and ocean currents. His hundreds of inventions included the lightning rod, bifocals, and the Franklin wood-burning stove. He designed ventilation systems for public rooms. Among his social inventions were the volunteer fire department and subscription library.

Monticello was Thomas Jefferson's personal laboratory. He experimented endlessly with crops, made an archeological report on an Indian mound he discovered on his property, invented a calendar clock and a revolving door, and designed the campus of the University of Virginia. As a young man he was fond of the violin and for several years played chamber music with his colleagues. Even now naturalists are impressed by his *Notes on the State of Virginia*, a book written for Europeans.

Thomas Paine wrote a treatise for Napoleon Bonaparte, recommending that the French people cultivate a native American plant, the potato. He also conceived of a smokeless candle and a vehicle with a combustion engine fueled by gunpowder. An iron bridge he designed was the first structure of its kind.

In *The New Story of Science* philosopher Robert Augros and physicist George Stanciu quote a number of physicists on the links between science and esthetic experience. Richard Feynman spoke of the beauty and simplicity of scientific truth. Heisenberg was immediately persuaded of the rightness of quantum mechanics by its "abstract beauty."

Henri Poincaré insisted that the nervous system scans for elegant solutions. "The useful combinations are precisely the most beautiful. . . . If nature were not beautiful, it would not be worth knowing—and life would not be worth living."

Max Planck, whose discoveries opened the way for quantum theory, said that new ideas are not generated by deduction but by an "artistically creative imagination."

Nobel laureate geneticist Barbara McClintock said that basically everything is one. "There is no way to draw a line between things." The subdivisions invented by human beings are not real, she said. "I think maybe poets have some understanding of that."

Jacob Bronowski, writing about what he called "the common sense of science," seemed to agree.

We seek to find nature one, a coherent unity. This gives scientists their sense of mission, and, let us acknowledge it, their esthetic fulfillment: that every research carries the sense of drawing together the threads of the world into a patterned web.

Artist as Scientist

Art is a venerable way to discover the patterned web. It seems to be part of our oldest nature, as much the human hallmark as toolmaking. Paleolithic paintings and the earliest glassmaking show that the human family has been creating art since we first found our hands.

In 1936, while listening to a lecture, Jonas Salk had a visual insight that led to the first effective polio vaccine. "It was almost as if the light was turned on and everything became clear."

And Salk said what many visionaries have thought but rarely voiced.

> Intuitions like that don't just happen once. It's like the circulation of blood, like brain waves. It's like the heart beating. People who are intuitive will draw conclusions on what they perceive to be a pattern. I wasn't taught this. I discovered it.

Take note: *He discovered the process of discovery.*

The best artists have the rigor and objectivity of a scientist. Bach spoke of "the science of my art, the art of my science." Composer Alexander Borodin was, in fact, a chemist whose experiments sometimes stained his music manuscripts.

Playwright William Coleman points out that Edgar Allen Poe anticipated the Big Bang Theory in a scientific treatise called "Eureka." "Poe proposed that the universe began with the explosion of a "primordial particle."

Diana Vandenberg, a Dutch artist, spent decades refining oil-painting techniques she developed after studying the methods of Leonardo da Vinci. Scientists have pointed out that some of her symbols are molecular structures. The director of an observatory wrote to tell her that she had chosen to paint an obscure constellation that had captivated astronomers as well.

The notion that visionary artists anticipate scientific discoveries is, of course, nothing new. Tennyson dreamed of battalions in the air. In our time military officials have quizzed science fiction writers about their sources. The invention of the communications satellite was inspired by science fiction writer Arthur C. Clarke.

Mythoscience

Some scientific findings are so stunning they become what we might call mythoscience. Such discoveries enter popular consciousness full-blown—a new version of How It Is. The paradigm doesn't shift; it jumps. Mythoscience is not necessarily understood, but the findings ring a bell.

We are fascinated but somehow not shocked to hear that there is a physical basis for human bonding, and that the brain produces its own painkillers. The near-death experience has become part of mythoscience.

Mythoscience makes radical common sense. When we tune into the information, it strikes us as essentially true. It strikes a common chord.

Speaking of "the dizzying development of science," Vaclav Havel cited the Gaia hypothesis and the Anthropomorphic Principle. The Gaia hypothesis maintains that Earth is a self-regulating organism. The Anthropomorphic Principle states that the conditions necessary for the evolution of life on Earth were extremely narrow, which calls into question the idea of chance. Havel said, "Both of these ideas remind us of what we have long suspected, of what we have projected into our forgotten myths—we are not here alone nor for ourselves alone."

10 FINDING THE RIGHT ENGAGEMENT

The Sacred Warrior

There are two wars, the Little War and the Great War.
The Little War occurs in the world.
The Great War occurs within you.

—ISLAMIC SCRIPTURE

The bells of the Earth have tolled long enough for death.
Let them now ring out for life.

—SEAN O'CASEY

Historical and mythical warriors find their strength and integrity by defeating their inner demons. The warrior is committed to a cause. The warrior fights for the cause and against those who would block the path or undermine the cause. Diplomacy is always the first move of a response to conflict. The warrior is a protector and a destroyer, not a conqueror.

It may seem strange to be calling on radical common sense at a time when some would be calling in the marines, but remember, our forefathers fought a war in which their mother wit prevailed.

We live in a different age, of course, and we cannot take arms against a sea of troubles. Leaders and governments cannot be brave on our behalf. A failure of courage all around is somehow part of our problem. Doing the right thing is rewarding in and of itself. Warriors do not look for credit.

How brave would we be if our lives and property were on the line? Would we join together to wage a guerrilla campaign? Would we have the courage to say with Patrick Henry, "Give me liberty or give me death"?

Courage: A Passion for Purpose

The word courage derives from the French coeur, meaning "heart." Courage is a force of the heart-brain, or limbic system. Brave comes from the word for barbarous and was originally used by the Romans to describe the courage of the "wild people."

Courage is the willingness to embrace challenge. It isn't a single trait so much as a combination of components: willingness, persistence, motive, bravery.

Real courage isn't boastful or reckless. It looks reality in the face. When change is called for, it accepts the need. It calculates whether the risks involved are commensurate with the goal.

When Julia Butterfly Hill was twenty-three, she climbed 180 feet into an ancient redwood. She lived in the tree for two years, saving it from loggers, and inspired a generation of environmental activists.

Awakening Warriors

The inner warrior can be awakened when we are confronted with situations that endanger ourselves or those around us. Many heroes have been taken by surprise. These sudden warriors were not anticipating confrontations.

A young soldier in China was sleeping on a bus when he was awakened by a commotion. Several hooligans were demanding money from a young woman. When she refused they threatened to strip her and throw her out the window.

Without hesitation Xu Honggang shouted at them to free the woman. They descended on him, stabbing him fourteen times until his guts spilled out.

Leaving a fifty-meter trail of blood, he pursued them down the highway. At first he refused treatment for his injuries.

> I don't consider myself a hero. I am still a son of the people in the Wmeng Mountain area and an ordinary soldier.

He declined an offer for a ride home, and on the train gave up his seat to a woman carrying a child.

Bullies have mastered the art of bluffing. Because they're seldom confronted they grow bolder, but a spunky opponent can send them on their way.

Lucky Babcock is an example of a spontaneous warrior. Looking out a window she saw a man throw a twenty-three-year-old woman to the pavement and rip off her blouse. Lucky, then sixty-six years old, grabbed her cane, flung open the door, and raced down two flights of iron stairs.

"I felt like I was flying. I put my hands on the rails and just threw myself down four steps at a time." She wielded her cane like a billy club and drove the man off.

Some people are signed-up warriors on a mission—going after particular causes. Raoul Wallenberg, a young Swedish diplomat, was sent into Budapest in the summer of 1944 to rescue Jews from the Gestapo. At that time the Swedish government issued only fifteen hundred passports a year. Wallenberg began printing counterfeits as fast as he could. He set up safe houses all over Budapest festooned with Swedish flags and guarded by blond Jews in Nazi uniforms.

Once he planted himself in front of a family to keep them from being shot. Another time he raced alongside a slow-moving train, opened an air vent, and dropped in the phony documents. Then he boarded the train and commanded the troops to release all the "Swedes."

Some people are natural warriors, forever doing battle against injustice. When Margot O'Toole was a junior researcher in molecular biology she raised questions about the validity of a colleague's paper. Crucial data had been faked, she said. After she was vindicated years later, her mother told a reporter: "She's always had a level gaze, if you know what I mean. If she wanted an answer from you, you'd better give it or she'd challenge you. It was honesty whether it was practical or not."

Her mother recalled an earlier incident when Margot was hurrying back from lunch and saw a slight man being beaten by a robust assailant.

She came trotting up sideways to the large man and said, "Well what do you think you are doing?" He said he was a detective making an arrest, but he had no badge. Margot collected names and took the matter to the authorities. The officer was suspended for a year.

A Persistent Warrior

Texas resident Marcelino Benitez learned from his mother in Mexico that his fourteen-year-old sister had been captured as a sex slave and taken to the United States by a man named Ramirez. Someone gave Benitez a photograph of the culprit and told him that Ramirez owned a restaurant in Los Angeles. Benitez headed west.

Going through the Yellow Pages he ordered food and asked for the names of the people who helped him. Next he took to the streets checking out restaurants all over the county.

He feared that going public would alert his sister's captor. Instead he canvassed between three and four hundred stops. At first he wasn't going to check out Mom's Bar B-Q, thinking it was closed, but then he saw a face inside that he recognized from the picture. To be sure he asked a passerby to place an order and get the name of the manager. It was Ramirez. He called the police.

His sister was frightened, but she was alive and now safe. A reporter commented on Benitez's accomplishment:

He had the air of a man who had simply done what needed to be done. He had walked into a metropolis with dozens of police departments, thousands of social service agencies and millions of strangers—and managed to take the law into his own hands without violating it.

Fine-Tuning a Warrior

A motorcyclist was riding up an unfamiliar rugged mountain pass in Yugoslavia. As he got higher and higher, the winter weather grew worse, the road more broken, and the precipice more frightening. But he could not turn back.

After a period of sheer terror, he realized that he'd been concentrating on the gaping holes in the road. He began scanning for good surface areas instead.

His entire experience changed. Within a short while he made it to the top and stumbled into an inn, whose hosts were astonished to see a guest in the middle of a blizzard.

When we become more involved in a project or a destination, we're often subjected to a variety of crises. We get our sea legs in meeting these challenges. We become more confident in our ability to handle the turbulence. Gradually we learn to take advantage of the unexpected.

Peaceful Warriors

Compassion is motivating. The truly committed develop a passion for compassion. The compassionate are the true keepers of the Earth, moved enough and indignant enough to take up the sword or the pen to wage war on injustice and incivility.

Gandhi and Martin Luther King, Jr. have been called peaceful warriors for having led nonviolent revolutionary movements with almost no violence on the part of protesters.

Mikhail Gorbachev was a great political warrior. His line of thinking unraveled the ropes that bound hostages in numerous nations, giving them an opportunity to rise up against tyranny and oppression.

George Black, foreign editor for the *Nation*, praised Gorbachev, along with Vaclav Havel and Nelson Mandela:

> These are politicians in whom substance takes precedence over style; all three are engaged in historical

struggles . . . Both Havel and Mandela have been persecuted and jailed for their political beliefs.

An interviewer asked Mandela if he was bitter about his
decades in prison:

To go to prison because of your convictions and be prepared to suffer for what you believe in, is something worthwhile. It is an achievement for a man to do his duty on earth
irrespective of the consequences.

An example of a nonpolitical compassionate warrior is
John Scherrer. A former schoolteacher, Scherrer was looking for
something productive to do. He invited a group of friends over
to discuss the possibilities. Everyone there was unmarried, so
they first called themselves "Singles for Charity," but success,
publicity, and a few marriages within the group inspired a
name change to L.A. CAN.

His innovative approach, networking volunteers and projects, achieved national attention for its simplicity.
Organizations let Scherrer know their needs for volunteers, and
his members check in to pick a job. They might find themselves
painting a shelter, hanging decorations for a benefit, stuffing a
mailing for the Special Olympics, or assisting CPR trainers. "It's
a wonderful way to help," one volunteer said, "and a way to
work with so many great people who want to help."

And Mother Teresa, whose work among the dying was
honored with a Nobel Peace Prize, typically told unhappy people, "Go out and help the poor. You'll forget your problems."

Whistle-Blowing

I don't want yes men working for me even if it costs them their jobs.

—W. C. FIELDS

Whistle-blowers are a unique breed. In honoring their courage
we strengthen our own resolve to resist the undertow of
collusion.

As early as 1969 toxicologist John Olney of Washington University reported that the popular flavor enhancer, mono-sodium glutamate (MSG) damaged the brains of young mice. He campaigned to get the substance banned from baby food.

Within a year after manufacturers had agreed to remove the chemical they had reintroduced it in the form of hydrolized vegetable protein. It took another seven years of hearings and protests before they took it out. Presumably the manufacturers added it to the baby food to make it more appealing to mothers.

Consciously or unconsciously, a number of people around the world seem to have little concern for the fate of the planet, actively doing things that contribute to our ecological failure. For a long time, corrupt corporate leaders and their collabora-tors have been selling products that harm people, knock sup-port away from those who are weak, and poison the environment. They seem to support or distort to their own purposes any theory or rationale that might justify their behavior. We're often scandalized by the tales of graft, yet every week seems to bring worse stories of greed and heartless-ness. We need to turn around the perception that nothing can be done about giant industrial lawbreakers.

In 1994, Erin Brockovich, a single mother of three working in a California law firm, discovered some medical records while looking through a real estate file for her boss. Knowing the medical records had nothing to do with real estate, Brockovich investigated and found that Pacific Gas & Electric Company had been buying up vast quantities of real estate in Hinkley, California, to cover up the fact that over a period of forty years they had dumped 370 million gallons of cancer-causing chemicals into the town's ponds, polluting the ground water and the aquifers that supplied the residents' drinking water. Brockovich and her boss defended the town's plaintiffs against PG&E in court and brought about the largest settle-ment on record for a civil class-action lawsuit.

People who seem to be without conscience tend to cross paths and do business together, colluding creatively, thereby having a synergistic effect. The bribers find the bribees. The companies into price fixing know each other well enough to agree on the numbers. The pharmaceutical distributors know the doctors who are willing to prescribe unnecessary drugs to children for a cash kickback.

For whatever reason the master advantage-takers gravitate together to do their mischief more efficiently. Yet there hasn't been such high-level affiliation between the wise and good-hearted. Whistle-blowers in every field are still punished. Those who lift the veil place themselves in danger. Alleged offenders have been known to intimidate, weaken, punish, even murder their accusers.

"The Jersey Girls," four women whose husbands died in the attack on the World Trade Center, waged their own fearless investigation into the events leading up to September 11, 2001. They refused to accept official assurances that government officials and agencies had no prior warning. They brought dereliction-of-duty charges against the President, the Vice President, the National Security Advisor, and others. Their efforts led to the establishment of the independent, bipartisan "9-11 Commission" that was charged with preparing a complete account of the circumstances surrounding the attacks.

As modern warriors, taking up our battle stations to fight for our vision or defend our values we can call upon our radical common sense. In this dynamic world inaction can be a fatal choice. In our decision to do nothing, we do something; we unconsciously block our natural caring.

Feeding the Visions

Once a purpose has taken hold, our resources tend to feed the vision. With a warrior's commitment to our chosen cause our radical common sense will suggest viable remedies and strategies.

Cathy Sneed, a prison counselor for the San Francisco Sheriff's Department, was in a hospital reading *The Grapes of Wrath*, John Steinbeck's classic novel about migrant workers in California during the Depression. Steinbeck had written:

A man might look at a fallow field and know, and see in his mind that his own bending back and his own straining arms would bring the cabbages into the light, and the golden eating corn, the turnips and carrots. And a homeless hungry man, driving the roads with his wife beside him and his thin children in the back seat could look at the fallow fields . . . and that man could know how a fallow field is a sin and the unused land a crime against the thin children.

When Sneed was told she was dying, she worried about her children and the prisoners she counseled. She remembered that when the jail was built in the 1930s there was a working farm within its walls. She told her boss, "We have to get the farm working again."

"If you get out of here, we will," he said. Sick as she was, swollen from her nonfunctioning kidneys, she walked out and started clearing the field.

She asked her children's elementary school teacher to come to the prison to teach gardening. "Cathy was so excited," the teacher said, "and so sick. And so insistent. Little did I know that she was the visionary who never gives up."

That was in 1984. Cathy Sneed didn't die after all, and the inmates of the San Bruno Jail now grow more than fifty thousand pounds of produce every year. On their release they "graduate" to a garden in one of San Francisco's troubled neighborhoods where they grow vegetables for restaurants.

Warriors have a way of turning negatives into positives.

During the Second World War, the residents of a poor French farming village—most of them descendants of Huguenots—conspired to save the lives of five thousand Jews.

Even officials of the Vichy government and German soldiers pretended not to see what was happening.

Pierre Sauvage was among those rescued. As an adult he returned to Le Chambon to interview the villagers for a documentary film, *Weapons of the Spirit*. They were surprised to be hailed as heroes. "We helped because they needed to be helped," they said. "It was only natural." For them there had been no choice.

Charles Schumer, the Brooklyn Democrat who led the fight to ban the sale of most military-style assault weapons, has been described by colleagues as a warrior. For Schumer being engaged is a fundamental value.

> Let me tell you a little story about the first job I had. I was running a mimeograph-duplicating machine. It was summer. I was thirteen or fourteen, and I'd get in there at nine a.m. A lot of my friends were out at the beach, or having fun. I'd look at my watch at 9:10. I'd look at my watch at 9:15. I'd look at my watch at 9:30. I swore I wanted to find a job that wasn't boring. This isn't boring.

A woman operating a beauty spa found she had breast cancer. At first she didn't want anyone to know. During chemotherapy her husband encouraged her that she could still look pretty. "Go out and show the world how to have cancer," he urged her.

She told her customers that she was fighting the disease, a move that clarified for her what was important. Five years later her cancer was in remission and she was speaking regularly to patients, inviting women to free seminars at her spa.

A newspaper editor in Uruguay who agreed to a duel with an irate police inspector announced that he would turn up without a weapon. He was challenged after his newspaper reported that cars registered in the officer's name had been seen carrying contraband from Brazil. "I am not going to bear arms against another human being."

He stood convention on its head. He gained the support of the press, many politicians, and much of the public. People were appalled that such a challenge could have happened in the 1990s. The exposure resulted in the transfer of power—a new president and party.

The Great War: The Struggle for Truth

Harry Truman once said, "I never give them hell. I just tell the truth, and they think it's hell."

Somehow the Great War—the war within—has to do with the nature of reality, our illusions and our perversion of it. The best weapon against any problem is truth. To the extent that we don't require truth, we'll continue to lie to ourselves. If silence means assent, unspoken truths are lies by omission.

The truth has certain advantages: It's easier to remember. It offers more opportunities for realistic improvement of the situation. It's disarming.

Truth emerges from unlikely places and people. Biologist Garrett Hardin once said:

> At no time are all of any society's beliefs correct. To improve itself—to move further from error and closer to truth—a society must have the guts to call on the crackpots to expose their thoughts to criticism.

Now and then a crackpot is right.

What if we waged a voluntary action on behalf of truth, a war against lies of destruction? Suppose we launched projects instead of missiles, if we fired off proposals and rejoinders, if we attacked injustice? What if we joined forces to overthrow the tyrants of our unconscious selves?

Writing in response to calls for armed resistance, Martin Luther King said: "Our powerful weapons are the voices, the feet, and the bodies of dedicated, united people, moving without rest toward a just goal." This is not to underestimate what we are up against, Dr. King said, "history has proven that social systems have a great last-minute breathing power, and the guardians of the status quo are always on hand with their oxygen tents to keep the old order alive."

"For evil to prevail, it's only necessary that good men do nothing," said Edmund Burke. If we don't protest when we are lied to by advertisers or when we see someone taking advantage of us, we're accomplices. What would happen if we started telling the truth? If we discussed our hidden agendas? Truth would eradicate dangerous myths, like technology as Messiah, or the lie that we achieve security through preemptive war.

If everybody who cared actually participated, the world would change. But we can't account for other people—just ourselves. If we do our part, who knows? And if we don't, who knows?

The task of the warrior is to persist in spite of the greatest opposition. Even if our efforts are in vain on one level, they keep us in the company of angels. Courage isn't risking ourselves for what we believe. It's letting go of the belief that there's something to risk.

11 CREATIVE RESPONSES TO FEAR

The Holy Fool

*Nothing in life is to be feared; it is only to be understood.
Now is the time to understand more, so that we may fear less.*

—MARIE CURIE

*I'm not afraid of the devil. I'm afraid of
people who are afraid of the devil.*

—TERESA OF AVILA

"Between the idea and the creation falls the shadow," T. S. Eliot said. It is the shadow, not a lack of ability, that is the obstacle to the expression of our best ideas.

The shadow spans the divide between what we want and what we get. It bridges distances between who we are and who we're meant to be, stretching farthest, widest, and deepest between the present crisis and our vision.

A shadow is created by blocking, deflecting, or intercepting light. Whenever a fear is born, it lives and grows and remains a part of us by positioning itself between the light of creation and our inner knowing.

Paranoia, worry, doubt, disease—they cast a spell at every juncture. Fear prevents us from seeing or feeling clearly. It blocks the natural flow of the rivers of senses and inhibits access to the radical.

Anxiety filters out solutions or paralyzes their implementation. When we do manage to get started, fear often calls us back at the first disappointment or sign of criticism. It depletes our energy. It prolongs our awakening. Fear gets us "stuck on stupid," causing us to repeat painful mistakes and lose sight of our common sense. We must get beyond this territory if we wish to uncover our visionary capacities.

Historically, creative people have felt separate from their societies—we might call it "the loneliness of the long-distance seer." It's as if they see too keenly the contradiction between what is and what could be. Innovators often find themselves isolated, with ideas and insights far in advance of the majority culture. The fear of isolation strikes a familiar chord in most of us. We fear that if we express our ideas, or act on them, others may withdraw.

"The visionary voice is the only thing that can save us at this point," Andy Lipkis, founder of the Tree People, said, "But people are afraid to follow their own ideas. They're sure other people will think they're crazy."

At times we all feel a little like the hero of Robert Heinlein's novel, *Stranger in a Strange Land*. We are harmed not by our uniqueness, but by our fear of being unusual. The Cult of Numbers, with its averages, means, and medians, encourages us to believe in something called "normal," which has little to do with being real. The notion of "average" or "typical behavior" is nothing more than mathematical convention.

Fear of Anomalies

Closely akin to the fear of being thought strange is the fear of information that disturbs our worldview. Talk of the so-called paranormal alarms many people. Because most of us were not taught about these phenomena in school, we resist the very ideas of telepathy, remote viewing, near-death and out-of-body experiences, precognition, mind over matter.

Psychologist Charles Tart found that fear of psi—psychic phenomena—existed in all the groups he studied, even parapsychologists.

The war being waged against parapsychology is more a matter of "killing the messenger" than a defense of reason. The fact is, there's precious little understood about nature.

An army task-force announced in 1993 that acupuncture, sleep-learning, biofeedback, hypnosis, and remote viewing were not effective. At the same time the army had top psychics on its payroll. It might serve us well to note that the debunkers—those who make it their business to discredit all forms of anomalous science—might be protecting hidden agendas.

On the other hand, many of us have shopped for cosmologies that are small, static, and understandable—junk theories. Life is uncompromisingly mysterious. There will always be anomalies.

Visionary people, with their usual practicality, take advantage of every byte of information, including the inexplicable.

Fear of Losing

Self-doubt assails us. It zooms in on the disparity between our preferred self-image and our insecurity. We're not thin enough or diligent enough. We're too late with too little. Such doubts make us hesitate, like drivers who cause accidents by being overcautious.

Time gets to us. We'll be late, we'll be early, we'll miss a deadline or a lucky chance. We'll fail to discharge responsibilities. We'll let people down just when they're counting on us. We're afraid we'll feel guilty.

Some fears are retroactive. Having been wrong is sometimes interpreted as having wasted one's time. One woman explained that she could not quit smoking because of all the years she'd spent arguing the issue with her mother.

A playwright recalls a period when he was afraid of losing his fear, and "then I'd be empty." Each of us has little patches of insanity. For example, a doctor was asked by a close friend why he kept a wall between himself and others.

"If I didn't, I'd feel weak."

"And what would that mean?"

Silence, and then sheepish laughter, "I wouldn't have the strength to hold up the wall."

Laughing at our irrationality helps. And we correct more readily if we think of ourselves as being on or off course rather than right or wrong. It's also comforting to remember that others can think we're wonderful without thinking we're perfect.

Sometimes we resist full awareness of our feelings. We don't want to bring those warning voices into the foreground. The trick is in distinguishing "the voice"—an identifiable, reliable cuing—from the inner chorus of second guessers.

Failure is a matter of perception. We can consider our disappointments in a tone of debriefing rather than one of despair. George Schultz, then secretary of state, was shuttling from one Middle Eastern capital to another in his quest for Arab-Israeli peace when a skeptical reporter asked what he could possibly hope to achieve.

Schultz admitted it was a long-shot mission, "But you can't be afraid of failing. What am I saving myself for?"

Most of us are probably influenced by the story-form of our culture in which the climactic scene leads to triumph or tragedy. Yet in real life we're seldom pitted against an antagonist, and there are few clear cut wins and losses.

Fear of Winning

Some people fear they are imposters, that they have succeeded only because no one has seen through them or caught up with them yet. If such success-fearing people are told that they have scored well on a test, their subsequent performance drops off enough to leave them in an "average" category. They don't want to succeed, but they're not willing to fail. Their goal is to be average.

Researchers have identified one important factor in the fear-of-success syndrome. Using a one-way mirror they observed the interaction of parents and children. The mothers and fathers had been told that the child was to perform a task and that they could help as little or as much as they wished.

The parents of the success-fearing children helped them a great deal, implying that (1) it was important that they succeed, and (2) they weren't likely to be able to do it on their own.

Some parents dread the success of their children. A sensitive child with a competitive parent may perform just well enough to get by without antagonizing anyone. An opera singer consistently followed her mother's advice to aim for second place, not first, so that she wouldn't be envied and isolated.

We may worry that success will harm our oldest friendships. Dorothea Brande pointed out in *Wake Up and Live* that most camaraderie is based on companionable grumbling. People who enjoy talking about the insurmountable obstacles to success don't take kindly to those who prove them wrong.

A pattern of success-avoidance points to early influences. Were we encouraged to shine, or did our family see success as something that came to other people? Some parents discourage excellence in favor of blending in.

Fear of Death

Fears are rarely fully conscious. Beginning in the 1980s the AIDS epidemic brought death anxiety to the foreground. Coming to terms with mortality awakens some of us to life.

Many eminent people have been narrowly spared prison execution, among them Arthur Koestler, Ernest Hemingway, Roberto Assagioli, Thomas Paine. Dostoevsky once said, "There is nothing that focuses the mind like knowing you are going to be shot at dawn."

In *Lost in the Cosmos*, Walker Percy made the point that suicide is a logical treatment for depression, and that depression is a reasonable state for thinking people. "One can acknowledge suicide as an option without electing to do it. 'To be or not to be' becomes a true choice."

Percy's term for those who have decided against suicide is "ex-suicide." He describes a non-suicide and an ex-suicide leaving the house for work at eight o'clock on an ordinary morning:

The non-suicide is a little traveling suck of care, sucking care with him from the past and being sucked toward care in the future. His breath is high in his chest. The ex-suicide opens his front door sits down on the steps; and laughs. Since he has the option of being dead, he has nothing to lose by being alive. It is good to be alive. He goes to work because he doesn't have to.

Novelist Colin Wilson observed that many visionaries he wrote about in *The Outsider* are defeated by their self-pity.

In his youth Wilson, intent on suicide, raised a bottle of hydrocyanic acid to his lips.

"I" felt I was standing beside a silly little self-pitying idiot called Colin Wilson who was about to drink this acid. And "I" didn't give a fuck whether he did or not because he was such an idiot. On the other hand, that would kill me too, and that was serious.

He suddenly switched identity. For three days afterward Wilson was lighthearted. He was two people, "and the one having all the troubles and miseries was not 'me.'"

Many people describe great bursts of productivity as well as surprising recovery after the diagnosis of a life-threatening illness. They were changed not so much by the diagnosis but rather by their altered concept of death.

The imminence of death can be immensely unifying. It's as if the community of subselves, like a town under siege, forget their trivial issues and pull together.

Researchers found that people who had a near-death experience tend to lose their fear of dying. In a classic NDE, people find that they are outside their physical bodies, looking down at themselves on an operating table or lying injured. They describe detailed activities at the hospital or at the scene of their accident. Many find themselves moving through a tunnel toward light, often seeing relatives and friends who died earlier. Interestingly, those who had attempted suicide say they would never again try to take their own lives.

When death is seen as a transition rather than an end, life takes on new meaning. Although there's no bottom-line consensus on the meaning, no one doubts that these experiences profoundly affect the "survivors."

An outstanding educator attributed her achievements to a wordless pact she made twelve years earlier as she lay dying of a stubborn staph infection.

She felt her life slipping away. Suddenly an eagle appeared in her visual field and expanded until it filled the room. Then she found herself in a dark tunnel. She knew that she was dying, and she didn't want to leave her ten-year-old son.

> So I made some kind of bargain. I had no idea just what I was promising but I know now that it was the work I'm doing. All of a sudden I was back in the hospital room, and the eagle was sitting on my left shoulder. It pierced me in the left eye, or so it seemed, and then it disappeared. From that day I've had sharper vision in my left eye than the right.

She gained a sense of purpose, however vague at the time, and a humble appreciation of death as a doorway.

It isn't feasible to schedule a near-death experience so that we can live more vividly and meaningfully. But we can pay more attention to how we're living and thinking. Are we postponing what we mean to do? We can open our eyes and see that this world is not long for this world. That might shock us into action.

Norman Cousins pointed out that we fear the wrong thing. "The great tragedy of life is not death but what dies in us while we live." Eighteen centuries earlier Roman emperor Marcus Aurelius wrote, "It is not death that a man should fear; he should fear never beginning to live."

Fear of Fearlessness

Many people see fear and worry as safeguards. If we were unafraid, what foolish or dangerous thing might we do?

A primal alerting response—the clear sense of danger at hand—has obvious value. It makes sense that warning pangs cause an emotional contraction. After all, most poison tastes bad. Our senses discriminate. Vigilance is an evolutionary asset we share with other living creatures.

Yet our brains can maintain a level of vigilance without the volatility of fear. As a sentry, vigilance is less trigger-happy.

"Don't fear fearlessness," the Dalai Lama told many audiences during a world tour. Fear is a blackmailer whose bluff must be called.

Worry has been called "a kind of pagan prayer." Having noticed that most things we fear never come to pass, many of us cling to a childish superstition: Worry and all will be well. We propitiate the gods by being unhappy well in advance of trouble. In many cultures people forego celebrations lest the gods become jealous.

Fear of Loss of Control

A lust for control may be our core addiction. We want our safety guaranteed. We think every possible precaution must be taken against a surprising turn of events.

In *Zen in the Art of Archery*, Eugen Herrigel points out that the archer's aim is more accurate if he doesn't attempt to control it. Star athletes and performers affirm this principle. Training and motivation are important, but before the great race or song or scene, they drop the concern for the outcome. They have prepared as thoroughly as possible and thus they are at peace.

There is a subtle difference between being in command and being in control. Controlling all the variables is impossible, but we can command our own reactions. Real power isn't having your way. It's in choosing your response.

"Fear forward," the saying has it. Visionaries often say that they are not unafraid; they just don't let their fear stop them. Psychotherapist Susan Jeffers captured this attitude in her book, *Feel the Fear and Do It Anyway.*

The Visionary as Holy Fool

We need to clear the channel to our higher guidance. For too long the still small voice of our inner prompting has been drowned out by the noise and commotion made by unwanted and unhealthy intruders.

Occasionally we were able to hear through the crowd and pick up the signal that beckoned to follow a higher directive. But quickly we'd give in to the jeering crowd and ignore the message once again. Before we exorcised our fears and phantoms, ghostly critics told us we were not good enough or we'd never have what it takes—or worse yet—that we'd make fools of ourselves.

Most of us dread being thought of as a fool, yet there exists a related archetype venerated in many traditions. In medieval Russia "Fools for Christ" were deeply revered. Buddhism has its "Crazy Clouds."

The notion of "crazy wisdom" appears in Hinduism, Tibetan Buddhism, Sufism, and Hasidic Judaism. In the medieval Rosicrucian tradition the Fool represents the highest achievement. The Fool in the tarot corresponds to the inner voice.

In the realms of business, sports, and politics, the Fool is a risktaker who mysteriously keeps learning and surviving. Ted Turner was labeled "crazy" by many when he launched the first all-news network, CNN, when he bought MGM, and when he staged the Goodwill Games in Moscow.

Turner made headlines again years later. There was little criticism of his style this time. Perhaps his reputation of success preceded him. Newspapers later romanticized his unorthodox approaches. One source even referred to his famous "zig-zag" method in a headline.

While campaigning for office, Florida's former governor, Lawton Chiles, worked at a different job every day for a year. As governor he set the bureaucracy on its ear by declaring a "state of emergency," authorizing all state employees to use their intuition rather than rigidly hewing to policy.

Holy Fools remind us that there are other ways of being and doing. An elder calling herself "Peace Pilgrim" walked more than 25,000 miles on a personal pilgrimage for peace, vowing to "remain a wanderer until mankind has learned the away of peace, walking until given shelter and fasting until given food." In her twenty-eight-year pilgrimage, she met and inspired thousands of lives.

Holy Fools and Practical Faith

Just as there are extremes in the weather, there are storms in our cultural climates—outrageous wars and unprecedented truces, governments reforming and ones undone by scandal, economic optimism and homelessness. At one and the same moment we seem to be lifted up toward a spiritual renaissance and dragged down by atrocities.

It's easy to get swept up in the polarized conflicts our media promote and dramatize. It's a more demanding task to see the good news. Sometimes it's subtle, sometimes it's disguised as calamity, but surely we don't want to be so busy looking for The Answer that we can't see the myriad solutions all around us.

Some people insist that nothing need be done, that world transformation is under way. "It's all happening anyway!" Such complacency is both naive and disempowering. Just as our liberties are only meaningful if we exercise them, spiritual renaissance is an opportunity, not an end in itself. Awakening is not a spectator sport.

Going with Our Inner Knowing

If we're to be responsive to this age we cannot choose between a life of reflection and a life of action. Both are essential. We have to act and reflect simultaneously. We can't afford the luxury of either-or.

There are many ways to bring about a better world, and we can experiment. Looking to Holy Fools as examples we won't have to understand everything we're doing so long as we're guided by our radical common sense. The more we follow this natural guide, this intuitive resource, the livelier we become.

In this turbulent time it helps to remember powerful metaphors. Consider Ilya Prigogine's model of large perturbations of energy that cause living systems to fall apart and then reorganize at a more elegant level.

Our present falling apart can be better dealt with if we see our social structures as a system. Whenever a group tries something new there's an inevitable period of chaos. Many people, mistaking the turbulence for the change itself, decide they prefer the bad old days and go back to the familiar dysfunction.

When we do that, when we run counter to our gut knowing that difficult changes must come, we rationalize our cowardice. "Better the devil you know," we say, "than the devil you don't know." And so we cast out the world that might have been.

Maybe this passivity is itself the devil it fears. It pretends to be our ally but it's really a tormentor. It withholds support we might have given to good causes. It says, "Wait and see," and thinks itself clever to have known that so many social visions would fail. The timid part of ourselves fails to realize that solutions might succeed if more of us participated. Seeing and doing are joined at the bone.

If we allow ourselves to be led by a collective higher spirit we can never really lose. We can let go of right and wrong, winning and losing, approval and disapproval.

The new world that's dancing now like a vision in the night can only be realized by us personally. It can't be designed, legislated, or ordained by institutions.

The new age that has been hovering over us for a very long time has nothing to do with the calendar and everything to do with being awake, and we have heard it speaking all our lives:

"*Carpe diem.*" "Seize the day." "Go for broke." "Walk your talk." "Try your wings." "Do unto others. . . ."

It's time.

12
LIBERTY AND THE LAW OF LEVITY
The Free Spirit

*The Divine upon my right impels me to
pull forever at the latch on Freedom's gate.*

—MAYA ANGELOU

For now we see through a glass, darkly; but then face to face.

—1 CORINTHIANS 13:12

Beyond the prison of our fears we see more clearly how unclear we've been.

"Personal sovereignty" was at the core of the old Celtic religion, and sovereignty seems to be a major issue for all of us. Who, or what, rules us? If other people make all the important decisions we might as well be feudal serfs.

As surely as we are breathing oxygen we breathe in our culture, even our family culture. On the other hand, it's suicidal to go along with the wholesale follies our society is pursuing.

No one has time enough to become conversant with all the overlapping systems that make up "the System." We are biological systems living in ecosystems and experiencing weather systems. Society is a merry-go-round of educational, medical, industrial, political, and communications systems. At the root are the systems of thought that help shape and sustain our society—our philosophies, psychological theories, cosmologies, and creeds.

We forget that people much like ourselves cooked up and implemented every policy that joined with other policies and beliefs to make up the institutions.

C. G. Jung once said, "Thank God, I'm Jung and not a Jungian." Relying on an adopted system we are like the painter's apprentice who saw the scaffolding in place and mistook it for the building.

Radical intelligence develops as we expand our knowledge of systems in general. Sometimes the answers come from the perspective of what we might call the holosystem. The holosystem includes the prison and the world beyond its walls.

Whatever form of slavery or dogma we find ourselves in, we can only be freed by a leap of faith—the faith that we can make it. To sense that we are somehow architects of our reality, or at least colluders, keeps us at the drawing board of vision.

Become What You Admire

One way to make the leap is to follow the Dalai Lama's advice: "You become what you admire. It's a very efficient way to change."

Admiration amplifies energy. It is a form of tuning in, an effortless attraction. Envy, on the other hand, is tuning out. Envy compares, jumps to conclusions, misses the boat and the moment. And let's face it, a competitive thought is not surprising after a lifetime in the Cult of Numbers. But if we notice the twinge of envy we can remind ourselves that we have an alternative—admiration.

We don't try to become the person but rather to take on a trait, like honesty, courage, or tact. We are homing in on a quality of being, a dynamic field that influences our behavior more powerfully than formal instruction. This is radical common sense.

The root of the word *admire* is a clue to the principle of attraction. *Ad-mirare*, "toward wonder," derives from a word meaning to smile or laugh. Admiration is akin to our delight when someone does something unexpectedly well. We can delight in the performance or handiwork of another—a breathtaking Olympic diver, a clever mechanic, a loving parent. When an agile mind plays with our own, when generosity or courage moves us to tears, we can be changed by fully experiencing our admiration. Unless, of course, we lose the moment because we're too busy wishing we were as smart or kind or brave.

Most of us are a little afraid to feel kindred to greatness. Yet how else can we aspire to our highest? In an essay titled "The Uses of Great Men," Emerson pointed out that the purpose of greatness is not to inspire hero-worship but to demonstrate valuable new traits available to the many.

From Regret to Self-Esteem

In learning the straightforward art of appreciation and respect we need to turn some in our own direction. Most of us withhold credit from ourselves because we're not perfect. We tend to think of our missteps as black marks against us rather than mere discordant notes.

Regret, mild or intense, is an everyday emotion in the lives of most people. Because it is commonplace and familiar we don't think about its drain on our self-respect.

We should notice the fruits of our kindlier self-instructions. The day may come when we glimpse the point of a lesson before we have to go through it. "God doesn't want you to get punished," someone once said, "just to get smart."

Crazy as it seems, we have to remind ourselves that nobody is good at everything. Superman and Wonder Woman were the dreams of cartoonists. The movie heroes from our childhood turned out to be human and we forgave them; it's time we forgive ourselves for lapses from our superhuman standards. Our ideals should inspire us, not set us up for humiliation.

David Florey, a "C" student at his Los Angeles high school, achieved stardom when his team took first place at the U.S. Academic Decathlon in Dallas. He was also the highest single scorer at the Decathlon.

How were people to interpret David's previously low grades and high achievement on the decathlon? "The way I would like people to interpret it," he said, "is that grades are not life."

"He's a free spirit," said his coach. "That's why he's good. He'll never let anyone else define him."

The Freedom to Question

From ancient times societies have tried to teach behaviors that tend to make things better for the tribe, much as an adult imposes discipline on a child or a pet (don't touch, don't pee there, don't run into the street). Society imposes rules that precede individual understanding. These come from the group common sense. But times change and guidelines appropriate to one set of circumstances can become nonsensical or even dangerous after a while.

John F. Kennedy suggested that the political role of the real artist is to challenge the assumptions of a society.

[Those] who create power make an indispensable contribution to the nation's greatness. [Those] who question power make a contribution just as indispensable, especially when that questioning is disinterested . . . when power corrupts, poetry cleanses.

This world will be more to our liking as an ever greater number of people ask questions and talk about their truths.

Love of Liberty

Abraham Lincoln said that a nation's liberty is not safeguarded by its guns of war or its "gallant and disciplined armies" but by our "reliance on our love of liberty."

Thomas Jefferson said it eloquently: "Some men are not born booted and spurred and others born with saddles on their backs that they might ride them." In an early draft of the Declaration of Independence, Jefferson raised the issue of slavery, charging England with having initiated the abominable practice. That passage was deleted. "All men are created equal" was understood by the signers to mean that they were equal to the king. Eighty-seven years later that phrase provided the loophole for the emancipation of the slaves.

Historian Garry Wills points out that it was Lincoln's most audacious act. He knew full well that the pro-slavery signers of the Declaration and the Constitution never meant to include slaves. At Gettysburg he took his stand: "Four score and seven years ago our fathers brought forth on this continent a new nation, conceived in liberty and dedicated to the proposition that all men are created equal."

A new culture, a new day, and the inevitable paradigm shift. In other writings, Lincoln reveals that Jefferson had been an example to him in this presumptive leap:

> All honor to Jefferson—to the man who, in the concrete pressure of a struggle for national independence . . . had the coolness, forecast, and capacity to introduce into a merely revolutionary document an abstract truth, applicable to all men and all times.

In his final debate with Stephen Douglas he spoke of the eternal struggle between opposing principles.

> The one is the common right of humanity and the other is the divine right of kings. It is the same principle in whatever shape it develops itself. It is the same spirit that says, "You work and toil and earn bread, and I'll eat it."

Liberty and Duty: Which Came First?

"We tend to picture freedom without responsibility," says Benjamin Barber, "imagining that our democracy can run forever like some great perpetual motion machine without the input of civic energy." Liberty requires that we participate.

Our leaders need our help. So do our neighbors and future generations. Although we require a wide range of remedies for society's problems, profound solutions will come from simple understandings in the universal laws we have ignored. For example, complexity creates change and new principles emerge from the marriage of new elements.

And actions speak louder than words.

Liberty is born of action. Creative acts give birth to freedom. Kennedy spoke of an America that would "steadily enlarge cultural opportunities for all its citizens" and of a world that would be safe not only for democracy and diversity "but also for personal distinction."

This gets to the heart of the matter. Political freedoms give us the chance to create the lives we want and the world we want. They open doors and windows that we might live a vision, and if we are too passive to exploit those freedoms we might as well live in a totalitarian society. In fact, our lives are held hostage by our parenthetical attitude toward liberty. It is now a mere footnote where once it was a grand exclamation.

Anyone who gets involved in the political process, even at a local level—and sticks with it—knows that you can fight city hall, at least some of the time. There are statutes that give us the opportunity to demand hearings, to address our leaders, to be heard.

The infamous "powers that be" do not often have to reckon with these laws because they count on our usual indifference. Discovering our capacities to lead and create will help us strengthen our "inner" democracy and end the struggle of our competing selves. We may have to go up against an inner tyrant or a self with special interests.

We have to find out who is in the control room. Until we can begin to detect that part of ourselves that knows better—what Lincoln called "the better angels of our nature"—we're not going to find society, or our collective selves, a happy place. Society is the sum total of our assumptions and behaviors. The world can only change as we change. As we become more mature we might do more than just make it through the night. We might even flourish.

As greater numbers of us learn to befriend the better angels in our nature we might see an epidemic of maturing. This kind of maturity has nothing to do with years. It's an ever present option that can animate our lives at any moment.

There Is Only One Choice

How do some people dare to be so radically themselves? What grants them the courage to risk their reputations or resources? Maybe they're calm and eccentric because their families encouraged their eccentricity. Still, why then don't most of us break out?

Jesus had scant regard for convention, whether he was healing on the Sabbath or socializing with tax collectors, "wine-bibbers," and prostitutes. Thoreau, a violator of tax laws, passed on the strategy of principled civil disobedience to Gandhi, who made a career of carefully considered law-breaking and taught his people the dangerous art of nonviolent protest. Gandhi's example inspired Martin Luther King, Sr., and his son, and the American civil rights movement, and the beat goes on and on.

Let's consider the possibility that those people we call "free spirits" are just the tip of the iceberg, a clue to the visionary life.

Let's hear the phrase as a command. Free spirit! Find out all the places spirit is imprisoned in your life and do something about it. Notice. Espy the barbed wire, the forbidding towers, the bars, the guards, the subtle intimidations that stand between you and your freedom. Don't ask permission, don't argue with the towers, the wire, or the gatekeepers.

Free spirit is not reckless. It's wild in a primal creative way. As someone has said, "There is only one choice: Freedom. After that there are no choices." If we aren't free to follow our own best guidance we aren't free at all.

Early Christians who went singing to their deaths in the lions' den in the Colosseum stunned the Romans. What kind of faith could inspire such courage? The Buddhist monks and students who torched themselves with gasoline to protest the Vietnam War sent shock waves through the world.

Self-indulgence and apathy are not choices. Empathy and knowing what to do, like all virtues, flow forth from the fount of radical common sense.

Reclaiming Spirit

It's time to reclaim spirit, vision, and creativity. The American dream is not to leave our fellow citizens in the dust and achieve material wealth or social power. It is the freedom to act on our dreams, so long as we do no harm to others.

Too often we relinquish the fundamental freedom of envisioning our own lives. Not only do we hire leaders to fight our battles; we want entertainers, advertisers, and politicians to do our dreaming. A culture that does not dream is not free. "And so we find redemption through consumerism," remarked Norman Lear.

Lear quoted Stuart Ewen:

Market force has become the value system—and we have come to the point where advertising has become the primary mode of public address; the term consumer has become a substitute for the word citizen—and the truth is that which sells.

It is precisely this issue that threatens our precious liberty in the twenty-first century. For out of apathy and fear we have allowed ideologues from church and state and the media to convince us of their authority. Demagogues prey on both our wishful thinking and our laziness. Much of what passes for authority and power is a bluff anyway, and it's time to call them on it. Free spirit is ready to move into every relevant realm.

Our ways are not congruent with freedom. That which is not conducive to creativity is not conducive to liberty, and vice versa. You can have control or you can have creation but you can't have both.

Freedom from the Control Police

We have been hostage to a system defended by nothing stronger than precedent. We're caught by institutions and patterns that may have worked once but don't serve us now. The ultimate villain is not a tyrant or a group. It is habit.

We, all of us, keep pushing buttons and responding to buttons on a panel wired to an obsolescent power system. The system, once defined politically as "the divine right" of kings, is still distinguished as paternalistic concern. We don't have to define ourselves as Democrats or Republicans, liberals or conservatives. What is this malaise that has turned us against each other? Why do we blame others? Even those charged with corruption or misbehavior were produced by a system woefully lacking in radical common sense.

The survival-oriented function of our brains, vigilant to a fault, is notoriously myopic. Research has shown that the right hemisphere grasps wholes and responds to novelty, whereas the left is linear and deals with parts. Our failure to integrate these functions is the crux of the present crisis.

And crisis it is. We stand at a crossroads that will determine whether life on Earth will be heaven or hell—creative community or endless divisiveness.

A Radical Awakening

In *Who Will Tell the People*, William Greider presented compelling evidence that various entrenched groups have made a mockery of democracy. For example, he showed how the tactics of environmentalists and political reformers were co-opted by wealthy opposition groups who created their own tax-exempt foundations and outspent citizen efforts ten to one.

We are about to learn whether we can defy history, Greider says, or whether we are

> just another muscular nation-state. . . . The usual story of great powers is that sooner or later, when the glory faded, they sank into social decay and bitterness. That is the usual ending for a political system that persistently ignores reality and for a people who become alienated from their own values.

Emerson warned that a society that fails to provide spiritual education will ultimately become animalistic, and in *The Universal Schoolhouse,* James Moffett made a similar point. Moffett offered a radical remedy for our current blues—"spiritual awakening through education." Like Havel, he pointed out that we have all been trained to be cogs. "Education never had a mandate to ensure personal development. Yet how can we create a sensible society, especially in light of growing complexity, if our uniqueness and potentials are ignored?"

In 1990 Norman Lear addressed over eight thousand teachers at a National Convention on Education for the NEA.

> I have a deep concern for what I consider to be a deep reticence—in our culture generally, and in education in particular—to discuss what might be our most distinctive trait. I'm talking about the mysterious inner life, the fertile and invisible realm that is the wellspring for our creativity and morality. For want of a better term, one would call it the spiritual life of our species.

Many efforts to upgrade the curriculum have been thwarted by special interest political hound dogs.

Lear, a television legend, Greider, a political analyst, and Moffett, an educator, all looked at the interplay of politics and education. And put out the wake-up call with all the urgency at their command.

In *The Slaves Shall Serve*, James Wasserman adds his voice to the call saying that we have been "asleep at the wheel" and that our "very ability to think, debate, and rationally examine ideas is being worn down by an educational system the purpose of which is to produce empty-headed sensualists whose materialistic concerns keep them in a perpetual state of tractability."

The Romans destroyed their brains by drinking wine laced with lead. Will there be historians and archeologists to guess at our story? Will they blame the Decline and Fall on our soft ways, mercury-toasted brains, or maybe our brittle values?

Most great nations, Toynbee said, are destroyed from within rather than falling to a conqueror. Maybe we could convene a modest-size meeting of concerned parties and do the postmortem ourselves.

The Tribe of the Between

In *The Speech of the Grail*, Linda Sussman wrote:

> We live between paradigms, between the old science and the new science, the old religion and the new religion, the old education and the new education, the old ways of healing and the new ones, and so on.

The social pathologies of Western culture, she says, are symptomatic of the disorientation and doubt of our era.

> We are the tribe of the between. We are like Parzival who, once he has seen the Grail, no longer quite fits into the welcome company of the Round Table, yet does not know the way back to his future.

Edward Harrison of the University of Massachusetts said, "Each universe of beliefs unifies a society and provides common ground so members have a basis for understanding each other." Unfortunately, each universe mistakes its own view of the world for reality.

He makes the point that each society believes it is on the knife-edge of knowledge and looks back with pity on peoples of earlier times because of their ignorance. We forget that future generations will look back on us in the same way. And what they will pity us for is our infatuation with the physical model.

The very purpose of science, it would seem, is to help us ask more meaningful questions. An experiment is a practical test undertaken in the spirit of truth. A sense of experiment is part and parcel of radical common sense. Science becomes our ally to help us verify or reject certain premises that impact our lives.

We should not live as prisoners within these models we ourselves have created. Our present paradigms are unfinished, only interim explanations until the next new perspective comes along. "Nature is not only stranger than we imagine," said biologist J. B. S. Haldane, "but stranger than we can imagine." We are well advised to hold our assumptions lightly.

In China, dragons are often shown holding a pearl and gazing toward it as if hypnotized. The pearl contains the secret of immortality. By eating the pearl the dragon would become immortal.

But he is fascinated by the pearl. He loves the shiny thing, so he perishes. We hold, if not immortality, at least pearls of great wisdom, and we sometimes get lost in their glow and iridescence. As we become more comfortable with our power to make things happen, we can embody the principles. We can eat the pearl, so to speak. Rather than admiring our ideals we can begin to live them. Every last one.

13 REMEMBERING THE FUTURE

The Navigator

*The future is uncertain . . . but this uncertainty
is at the very heart of human creativity.*

—ILYA PRIGOGINE

*The history of discovery is full of arrivals
at unexpected destinations, and arrivals
at the wrong destination
by the right boat.*

—ARTHUR KOESTLER

It's time to remember our origins. It's time to remember the time before we became experts, before our subselves forgot how to act with radical common sense. This doesn't involve so much a list of how-tos or to-dos as it involves something called remembering the future.

How well equipped are we for the swift, unknown parts of the journey? Or the passages we have to execute in the night? To what extent can we shape what happens?

By now we have an advantage: our ability to navigate is grounded in our prior commitment. Our willingness to improve any situation makes it easier to take on bigger tasks.

Action means experience means lessons. As we acquire more history, remembering the past, we become more adept at predicting the future. We gradually learn the gambits for navigating around obstacles for a goal.

There is timing—waiting for a better opening. And there is determination—wearing down resistance. And there is persistence.

Experience is our most obvious navigational aid—an ever-better handle on the likelihood of a particular strategy working or not. The databank of our prior successes and failures offers guidelines for maneuvering. Efficiently stored information allows a complex search process to take place at lightning speed. This acceleration of insight into novel situations is the fruit of prior hard work—and prior noticing. When we don't have time to wonder if we can cope we simply call upon our best efforts.

As we seek novel challenges we develop new instincts. The instinct to live instinctively becomes a navigational aid that evolves as we evolve. It calls upon a deeper source of expert-ise—the ability to coordinate many functions into a single smooth movement.

Sometimes we perform acts for which we have no known preparation. We find ourselves operating a machine we've never seen before, or flawlessly playing a new game. In our navigational parlance we might call this access to the charts of earlier explorers, or we could call it remembering.

According to Rupert Sheldrake, a British plant physiologist, we're born connected. The prior learning of others can be tapped by way of an invisible matrix he calls the morpho-genetic field, or M-field.

In *A New Science of Life* he advanced this ground-breaking theory, saying that the structure and behavior of organisms is governed by self-replicating M-fields. "These fields program an organism's development through 'morphic resonance' via its genetic mechanisms similar to a television station program-ming a picture via the TV set." Sheldrake describes morphic resonance as the "basis of memory in nature . . . the idea of mysterious telepathy-type interconnections between organ-isms and of collective memories within species." We can take this to mean that we resonate with our past, our future, and the whole human race.

Sheldrake's hypothesis may also account for a number of puzzling phenomena observed in research. For example, although it is difficult to synthesize an organic compound for the first time, successive crystallizations are much easier to produce anywhere in the world.

Sheldrake's theory of morphic residence makes more sense than the conventional wisdom that "seed crystals" from the original labs were carried to other laboratories on the clothing and in the beards of the original researchers.

We're like the seed crystals: whenever one of us evolves, so do we all.

Choosing Our Emphasis

This leads to another navigational aid: Choosing our emphasis. We choose our filters. We can choose to remember our bad experiences and look for evidence that another one is in store. Or we can set our sights on a better outcome. The search mechanism is neutral. It scans on a look-alike basis, seeking a matching gestalt rather than random facts. Its genius and its vulnerability are in its guessing. What you choose is what you look for; what you look for is what you see; and what you see is what you get.

Self-fulfilling prophecies come true because we believe them. For example, if a candidate is rumored to be behind in the polls, voters hesitate to vote for him. If we're afraid that a friend will be angry with us, our discomfort upsets both of us. On the other hand, anything that triggers confidence seems to mediate success, as in the high expectations of teachers inspiring dramatic rises in children's abilities.

It doesn't take a wizard to realize that if a melancholy outlook produces a melancholy environment, then conjuring up a pleasant outlook is likely to generate a pleasant one. We can choose from among plausible outcomes. Focusing our expectancy on a favorable prediction unifies our efforts. We have nothing to lose. Even if the negative outcome manifests, we're in a better frame of mind to deal with it.

A ballerina describes her experience: "It happens like this: I think, what if I'm so tired I can't make that turn? And, worried about exhaustion, I go dead. My toes get weak, my feet get numb, my legs turn to jelly."

She says she has to get over the idea that she might fall or fail.

> It takes years to get to the point where you can fall back on your technique and relax about everything else. And when you're mentally free to draw on your inner resources, you can do more: You can balance longer, do three pirouettes instead of two, because you're not afraid to take a chance. You might be puffed, breathing hard, but you still have more energy inside you.

As Henry Ford once said, "It doesn't matter if you think you can or you think you can't. Either way you'll be right."

As the old saying goes, "The Lord helps those who help themselves." If we cope in good spirit with our troubles we'll become stronger in mental and physical muscle. Even the sense of having chosen our attitude can make the difference between life and death. Heart-attack patients who attribute their illness to their behavior or lifestyle are less likely to have a second one. Nursing home patients allowed to choose between dinner entrees or select the color of their curtains are healthier.

Even if we have little choice in the matter at hand, we can choose an attitude of acceptance, which at the very least gives us greater peace of mind. We can choose physical attitudes as well. When we slouch or cower we feel like a different person than when we hold our head high. Our gesture and posture alter our capacity.

Experiments have shown that if we deliberately put on a smile or a grimace while reading either humorous or negative subject matter, we tend to take in, and recall, the information that matches our facial expression.

The word *pretend* has a meaning other than just faking it. It comes from the Latin *pre-*, plus *tendere*, "to stretch." Pretending can be a powerful way to stretch oneself into action. In some esoteric traditions this technique is called "as if." We think and act "as if" something could be so.

By envisioning ourselves in greater service, planning, and acting as if the dream is inevitable we become what we beheld.

"They can," Virgil said, "because they think they can."

Sailing on the Wings of Grace

In recent years there's been growing interest in the "flow state" or "optimal performance." Flow isn't a new discovery; in olden times it was called "the state of grace." Time and self-consciousness seem to be suspended, obstacles fall out of the way as if by magic, old limits are transcended, details seem to handle themselves. There's immediate access to memory, and goals seem to be within easy reach.

Most have experienced grace, a few hours or a day when everything meshes, every errand is fruitful, and "the force" is with us. Inspiration seems to merge effortlessly with action. Then, as mysteriously as it came it evaporates, and we find ourselves once again in the world of fits and starts, hostage to our normal state—eaten at by vague regrets and worries.

The flow state proceeds from trust, an intention lightly held, and a playful spirit. These generate a sense of command. This acquired confidence frees us to deal spontaneously with unfolding opportunities, responding to the demands of the moment.

Grace is purpose in action, giving impetus to change. In the flow we can enlarge the context. Not just to do the right thing but the inspired thing.

Psychiatrist M. Scott Peck describes the phenomenon:

Are we to ignore this force—grace—because it doesn't fit easily with traditional scientific concepts of natural law? The call to grace is a promotion, a call to a position of higher responsibility and power. It brings paradoxically peace and responsibility. Grace is total adulthood.

We can achieve the state of grace more readily when we look to the present rather than postponing joy until some future good fortune. Tying fulfillment to the future is a subtle side effect of the Cult of Numbers.

Our quality of life is not determined by material resources but by our vantage point, our attitude, the place we look out from. Why can't we spend more time in the state of grace? Among the factors:

Guilt. Sometimes the state feels like cheating because things are "too easy." We miss the familiar struggle.

Fragmentation. A mental split. We can't experience the present moment if we're busy oscillating between hope and fear. Maintaining the split consumes energy.

Navigating requires that we notice our noticing. We attune to input that might otherwise vanish into the black hole of habit.

Peter Lemesurier, in *Beyond All Belief,* wrote:

We are all believers. Belief is the very tool with which we make sense of what, in our earliest years, necessarily seems to us a confused and chaotic reality. Yet possibly it is the child who sees the world as it is and we adults who use belief as a filter to help us see the world as we want to see it.

Lemesurier suggests that belief and knowledge are uneasy rivals. "The more we find out the more our cherished beliefs have to go overboard."

If we remember to check our intuition frequently we can create a new habit—the habit of staying awake. Little by little we train our brains.

Eventually we learn to align ourselves with what Hemingway called "grace under pressure." When we learn to experience challenges more as waterways to navigate than mountains to conquer, grace is a more frequent companion.

Remembering the Future

In *Life on the Mississippi*, Mark Twain wrote, "My boy, you've got to know the shape of the river perfect. It's all there is to steer by on a very dark night."

Knowing the "shape of the river perfect" in terms of mapping our past enables us to improve our future. One of the benefits is the discovery of lost truths. As individuals, we let certain skills get rusty just as civilizations lose sight of important knowledge. The secret of making concrete, for example, was lost after the high Roman Empire and rediscovered in the nineteenth century.

"To know nothing of what happened before you were born is to remain forever a child," Cicero wrote. Our collective history can serve as a guide, suggesting directions to take, or not take. In order to make intelligent decisions we must establish a connection with our past. And we must keep a vision of our future selves in focus simultaneously.

In *Alice's Adventures in Wonderland*, Alice is shocked by the idea of "living backwards." In astonishment she says, "I never heard of such a thing."

The White Queen says, "But there's one great advantage in it, that one's memory works both ways."

"I'm sure mine only works one way. I can't remember things before they happen."

"It's a poor sort of memory that only works backwards," the queen replies.

In *Culture and Commitment*, Margaret Mead wrote about navigation from the perspective of society.

> If we are to build a prefigurative culture in which the past is instrumental rather than coercive, we must change the location of the future . . . we must place the future . . . among us, already here, ready to be nourished and succored and protected.

We can notice the present by imagining ourselves in the future, a kind of future history. We can remember the future from the present moment.

Old sailors would tell us that the goal, or desired destiny, mobilized their navigational sense. Veterans of the sea remember that a clearly envisioned destination is a harbinger of speed and success. Navigation is a matter of perspective as well as directions and calculations. When it comes to making our way through the present crisis strong visionary powers become our only reliable sense.

W. W. Wager said, "The ultimate function of prophecy is not to tell the future but to make it."

The future is an environment for our creation. In Howard Fast's novella, *The Trap*, a group of gifted children are reared on a reservation by enlightened adults. In this ideal environment the children discover that by putting their heads together they can listen to each other's thoughts. Over time they become remarkably compassionate and function as a single mind.

Near the end of the experimental internment, the supervisors ask for another seven-year period. At the end of that time officials from Washington arrive for the emergence of these unusual individuals only to find—nothing.

A final letter explains the disappearance. The young people realized that they'd be a threat to the existing order because of their psychic and creative powers: Someone would want to eliminate them, and it would be against their principles to do battle. Therefore they moved a nanosecond ahead in time. They were still in the world but in an infinitesimally different time zone.

Perhaps vision offers an advantage, placing us at a tiny remove from conventional thought. Visionaries sometimes seem to move spontaneously in spirals rather than in predictable straight lines, quick and elusive. Maybe vision allows us to live ahead, one nanosecond into the future.

Andrew Leeds, a Los Angeles psychologist, used a technique he called "hypnotic future progression" to study precognition. His initial findings did not support the idea of the technique as a window into an objective future, "But they may shed light on some of the reasons for fears of global catastrophe," he said. Subjects who had undergone significant psychedelic, mystical, or near-death experiences reported more optimistic utopian future worlds. Those with limited peak experiences tended to foresee global catastrophe.

Remembering the future is nothing more than allowing oneself to imagine it so vividly that it's difficult to discern the vision from the memory. Once we see vividly our faith deepens. We can scarcely imagine failing. A trained imagination welds the elements together, giving greater concreteness to our goals.

Ingo Swann, an early remote viewing laboratory subject, broke with his own policy when a woman attending a keynote speech in Germany's Black Forest pleaded with him to make "just one" prediction.

In that moment he suddenly "knew" that the audience had the answer, and just as suddenly he startled himself by saying, "The Berlin Wall will come down within eighteen months."

The translator hesitated. Swann insisted, "Say it!" The audience upon hearing began applauding; then they started a standing ovation. Finally they stood on their chairs clapping and cheering. Swann recalls leaving the gathering in trepidation lest any of his colleagues should hear that he went out on such a limb.

"Imagine my surprise," he says, "nineteen months later as I lay on my bed in my apartment in New York, eating potato chips and watching the wall come down." Swann believes he "tuned in" to the unconscious of the members of the audience. Perhaps in that charged moment he also tuned into the minds of the movers and shakers whose actions would lead to the reunification of Germany.

David Loye of the Institute for Futures Forecasting tested 135 subjects including 64 students in the Naval Postgraduate

School in Monterey. He found that people with balanced brains—who do not have a strong dominance of either hemisphere—seem to be better able to anticipate the future.

Adapting and Flexing

Radical common sense supports the idea that once we know that we don't know it all, we can accept the likelihood that the impossible idea is possible.

The task of mind, said Nikos Kazantzakis, is to build a "seawall in chaos," to find the strands and patterns. When they feel confused visionaries seek more—not less—information. In other words, the answer doesn't lie in "hunkering down" but in further detective work. Some look for alternatives. A business leader and philanthropist said, "I 'blow up the picture.' I imagine the situation as an eight-by-ten enlargement, so I can see the details better."

"True intellectual growth," said Shirley Hufstedler, then secretary of education, "is always accompanied by a sense of surprise—the feeling of suddenly turning a corner and seeing a whole new landscape whose existence you never suspected."

Our breakthroughs come through the good offices of surprise. A fresh understanding empowers more effective thought and action.

Some people deliberately arrange for surprises in their daily schedules. The need to improvise builds muscle. Actor Paul Newman said that he rarely knew for sure what the next day would bring. "It's important to keep yourself a little off balance."

Saxophonist Paul Winter teaches people how to "consort"—to converse with one another through the use of musical instruments, emphasizing the importance of getting lost, again and again, until one is unafraid of the unknown.

"Planning is obsolete," said Larry Wilson, founder of Wilson Learning Systems. "The only thing to do now is navigate."

Navigation carries us into uncharted waters. We can think of recovery from mistakes as course-correction and simply get on with it. There are no absolute routes and the nature of water is unpredictable. Storms can be anticipated but not controlled.

The fool's sense of excess can be a valuable tool in learning to navigate. What are the parameters? If we never exceed them we'll never know.

Thomas Hohstadt, a composer and orchestra conductor, tells how a sense of incompleteness permeated his work despite "carefully analyzed immaculately precise and historically accurate performances." His feelings of unfulfillment led him to explore music more deeply.

> It's strange what happened next. A silly line from the Wizard of Oz kept running through my head. "Follow the Yellow Brick Road." Instead of techniques there were paths which not only gave permission to any outcome but required a total commitment much broader than playing an instrument, conducting an orchestra, or building a career.

Since then he has explored these paths and looked for new ones. He finally came around to the possibility of calling them techniques but with a different understanding of the word. These paths/techniques were nonrational. They were to be used on behalf of quality—not quality as understood by a cosmopolitan sophisticate but the quality of profound meaning.

They were "designed to lure the listener beyond these limits. We enable—we do not own or control—the meaning of music. Our techniques must serve a musical truth that springs only from the power to which it points."

Successful artists, you'll recall, are more interested in the process than in the final product. The attraction is to the navigation. We become more flexible on the journey and more resourceful. We risk. Our hearts are broken. We are sadder but wiser—and strangely happier.

When Albert Camus urged artists to come away from the sidelines and begin rowing the human boat, the vessel he had described was a slave galley. But if we're to help free our communities and nations to be more creative, the most intelligent move might be to build another boat—or a whole flotilla of craft—agile enough to escape the bondages of slavery altogether.

Inspiration Is Our Heritage

We would count a person seriously ill if he could not excrete or urinate, Colin Wilson points out in *The Philosopher's Stone*. "Why do we not count a man ill if his mind is dull and uninspired? Mystical vision should be as natural as excreting."

While we are climbing the evolutionary staircase, he maintains, we are all but immune to death. If we could come to see consciousness as it really is, active and relational, we would be inspired into immortality.

> A healthy consciousness is like a spider's web, and you are the spider at the center. The center of the web is the present moment. But the meaning of your life depends on those fine threads that stretch away to other times, other places, and the vibrations along the web.

Normally, Wilson says, our consciousness is like a very small web. Its threads don't stretch very far.

> Other times, other places aren't very real. And the turbulence of everyday life breaks the web. But sometimes the wind drops, and you manage to create an enormous web. And suddenly distant times and distant places are as real as the present moment, sending their vibrations down into the mind. . . . The pessimistic philosophers who find life meaningless are simply weaving a very small web.

Our chief human problem, the narrator in *The Philosopher's*

Stone says, "is our slavery to the trivial." He speculates that there is no such thing as death, there is only suicide. "We do not die of old age. We get fixed in old habit patterns until our capacity for 'otherness' is destroyed and then we allow ourselves to sink into death."

In other words, if we could snap out of habits we would never lose touch with the springs of life. This is a familiar theme in Wilson's writings, the power of consciousness to radically change the body and therefore the voyage.

There is such a thing as a view from a higher or deeper place. Our human gift is the ability to imagine such a place and know from there.

We can train ourselves to be optimistic, knowing that it helps. We can refrain from pessimism because we know that negative thinking works, too.

What seems universally important is trust. The highly innovative person learns to be comfortable with a general direction, not knowing much beyond the next step.

The more quickly we respond to cues, the more quickly we move on. We learn to see the openings. If we attune to the moment we'll make the right moves. The good life isn't lived in units (one minute, one hour, one day) but in experiences.

Jung said that understanding synchronicity is the key that unlocks the door to the totality we find so mysterious. The idea of synchronicity, psychiatrist Jean Bolen says, is unnerving in its implication that our lives are inherently meaningful and that we are therefore responsible to live that meaning.

> In the synchronistic moment the separate "I" no longer feels "How lonely it is." Instead, the person directly experiences a sense of oneness. This is what is so deeply moving in experiences of synchronicity and is why these events are often felt as religious, or spiritual. When we feel synchronicity we feel ourselves as part of a cosmic matrix. . . .

Synchronicities are quite common. Bolen suggests they represent an unfolding from what the Chinese call the Tao—the underlying unifying principle of the universe. The sense of something that was "meant to be."

Synchronicities seem to increase in the flow state. Barbara Honneger, then of Washington Research Center in San Francisco, suggested that synchronicities are the right brain's way of talking to the left. She kept a diary of synchronicities for seventeen years. She recommends the practice of tracking meaningful coincidences and other phenomena—telepathy, precognitive dreams—so they can be reviewed.

The intuitive right hemisphere, she believes, wishes to communicate unconscious needs and proposed solutions through symbolic language, events, objects, and "coincidences." The right has a rich and subtle understanding of language but is thwarted by its neurological inability to control speech and writing. Therefore it alerts the left brain by psi or involuntary attention to certain objects or information.

Veteran researcher Rhea White seeks to redefine the basic mission of parapsychology, the field in which she's spent decades working at the forefront. She urges an active investigation into visionary experiences and the people who have them.

She says recording unusual experiences

> is the most important first step one can take to help the world. . . . If you immerse yourself in your exceptional experiences and honor them, it's likely that more will occur until you find that you are a new person living in a new world, and you have lots of company.

Serendipity is do-it-yourself luck. Those who take pleasure in making the most of everything seem to enjoy more good fortune. Perhaps they have more energy because they are not resisting events. Or maybe they find treasures because they're looking.

Often when we are working to envision solutions we get a bonus—an uncanny knowing whom to call and when, what step to take. Something seems to prompt our every action, opening doors like an electric eye. We move beyond mere remembering into the past, present, and future simultaneously. Attention and intention merge effortlessly. We are at once the creator and the creation.

A Radical Rescue

Timing. Synchronicity. Serendipity.

It's no coincidence that so many curious souls were born at this moment in history when nothing short of an army of visionaries can save the world. We have the tools, the craft, and the crew to pull off a miracle here. The only thing we don't have is a choice. One obstacle we can't navigate around is the simple fact that we need a world to live in.

For most of history ambitious folk who betrayed the public interest for private gain could avoid the consequences by moving. People who stockpiled weapons and waged wars did not expect to fight or send their children to battle. For generations, perhaps for millennia, those who had the Midas touch could design their own escape routes. They could live on hilltops, in other neighborhoods altogether, or leave the country.

The American founders attempted to establish an egalitarian society, an ideal of opportunity and justice. In the context of the times their achievement was immense, but we'd be naïve to think they had attained their goal. In fact, they knew that the revolution had just begun.

We are now face to face with an enemy closer at hand than George III. As Gandhi once put it, "Your opponent is not the enemy. The problem is your enemy."

The enemy, simply put, is our failure to use radical common sense.

We can establish new frameworks for political freedom and they too will be twisted because we have not yet acknowledged that our psyches are unfree. The species will survive only if the entrenched interests recognize their own endangerment: when they realize that we're all in this thing together.

Only radical common sense can prevail. This boat is sinking. Sinking, not because of nature's storm or God's vengeance but because we are punching holes in it. We are—if you'll excuse the mix of metaphors—drowning in global warming. If you gradually destroy the ingredients of viability it doesn't matter if you're going to freeze or burn. You're dead either way. We've closed our eyes and ears for so long we've almost missed the point.

We can wake up. We can save this ship and we can create the kind of world our ancestors envisioned—and even created here and there for a moment. But it will require nerves of steel, a heart of gold, and a habit of perpetual renewal.

This is where the radical meets the conservative meets the liberal. To be radical means, literally, to go to the roots. To conserve is to save. To be liberal is to reform progressively.

We can turn this thing around but only if we learn to become a whole species by throwing away all the distinctions and calling together the troops.

We can turn this thing around if we remember the future as a collaborative effort. We design our vision in conjunction with events and in cooperation with the needs and hopes of those near and far. Remembering the future is energized by our prior willingness to follow through. This is radical common sense.

14 CREATING THE FUTURE
Reclaiming Our Sovereignty

*The eye makes the horizon. Morning comes,
and all across the sky I see signs of progress.*

—W. E. B. DuBois

The most holy form of theory is action.

—Nikos Kazantzakis

"There is no such thing as a genius," Buckminster Fuller once remarked. "Some of us are just less damaged than others." He expressed it a little differently on another occasion: "I'm convinced that every child is born a genius. Most are de-geniused by loving parents who are afraid the genius-inspired initiative of their children may get them in trouble with the going socioeconomic system in which they live."

The gap between human capacities and human realities is stark enough to make a stone weep.

Physicist David Bohm was preoccupied at the end of his life with a curious problem. Thought, he proposed, is the devil that got us into the present crisis. Thought designed our unworkable institutions. As Bohm saw it, only in dialogue—only in our social network—can we get the feedback crucial to high functioning as individuals. Together we can sort out what works and what doesn't. Bohm helped to create a network of dialogue. He put his theory to work. He tested the common sense of community, discoveries and strategies gathered from a number of people.

Bohm was right. We're only going to make it if we tune in to the larger community. That's our choice.

Virtual Royalty

The word *reality* derives from royalty. The very concept referred to a sovereign authority, not a collective perception. Little wonder that we lack a consensus on reality.

Nothing has changed except that the determiners of paradigms are sanctioned institutions governed by those who hold the highest cards. Power is dispersed in modern society and the royal-reality game is played out in many arenas.

Freedom in our democracy doesn't require that we mobilize against the divine-right crowd, the righteous hoarders of wealth and power, the belittlers and justifiers, the defenders of entitlement. There's a sensible alternative: To assume the rights and responsibilities of our own reality. To support the kingly and queenly qualities in ourselves and others—the divine right of everyone.

Inquiring into the origins of monarchy we learn that early kings did not bully or strategize their way into power. History suggests they were chosen by peers as the individuals best suited to look after the region. In other words they were trusted. Divine-right doctrine came later to justify passing the crown to descendants.

If we take on noble qualities and admire the nobility in others a more just order is established. We're all uncommon. Each of us is unique, we have destinies, we're born to be brave and intelligent. And if we're not yet all that, who's to say where our mission might take us?

Recognizing our royalty is a step toward ennobling others. That stranger, that annoying boss, that aimless teenager, all are heirs to a kingdom. Our brains and bodies are more elegant than palaces, and as the story of King Midas reminds us, love and life are more precious than gold.

Freedom begets freedom or it is no virtue. The monarch within is itself the free spirit, empowering and guiding the other selves, and giving birth to new ones in response to new needs.

These are demanding and chaotic times. We'll have to

make some improbable leaps. We won't know what's possible if we don't see discoveries, test hypotheses, and play.

We are born to play. Children play purposefully, as we can see by watching the dedication they bring to a game.

The Olympics of ancient Greece weren't staged for winning but for participation. When we approach our lives in a similar spirit, we emphasize dedication and enjoyment. "The difference between smart people and brilliant people," one visionary remarked, "is that brilliant people know how to play."

Remembering that it's a game frees us from regrets. If we're looking back at our failures we can't see where we're going. It's better to get whatever is their lesson and go on. As players we look at the game as part of the practice and the practice as part of the game. Looking ahead we anticipate the next move.

Serious play demands that we come to know the practical world, whose laws must be observed, and that we master our emotions, for we cannot hold a vision with shaky hands.

The more attracted we are to the game the stronger our allegiance toward our purpose. Commitment is an organic pull toward something that makes it easy to stay on course.

Engaged in serious play, we're so busy keeping our eye on the proverbial ball that we have no time for fretting or fearing. Only by taking on more than we can handle do we learn the rules of the game. Visionaries shoot for the stars to get to the moon. And they don't call it failure.

Serious players take their humanness into account when setting goals.

The Power of Sharing

Serious players rediscover the need for one another, not to accumulate knowledge but to gather the intelligence of heart and soul. I do my best, so you can do your best, so I can do my best.

We don't take power, we *are* power. What we take is responsibility. That's why players find and use their networks. Power isn't having your way, remember, it's having options and allies.

Players share resources, technologies, strategies. A new visionary game arises from a fusion of cooperative agendas. The alternative to competing is a dance of creative processes. This is where our sense of efficacy determines the road we take. We finally understand that there can be no winning and no losing because there never has been.

Sometimes we're so caught up in our specialties we fail to apply imagination to our own vocations. We're too familiar with how it's done to see a radically different approach. But we might have flashes of inspiration or insights into someone else's area of expertise.

These days we can only think in terms of rapid changes. We have to scrap the idea of relying on our conventional methods. We need to emphasize connections rather than boundaries between areas of knowledge. Radical common sense is a universal skill.

Nikos Kazantzakis once said our purpose is to get involved in the struggle, "not to look on passively while the sparks leap from generation to generation, but to leap and burn with it. Action is the widest gate of deliverance."

Action awakens the Self that is more than the sum of our parts.

Rules of the Game: There Are No Rules

For many years people have argued about priorities. Which comes first, reforming the world or ourselves?

The American Transcendentalists maintained that inner reform must precede outer reform. Considerable damage has been done by ill-prepared reformers whose intentions were better than their policies.

On the other hand, we develop our skills and gather knowledge in our social interactions. The world, in turn, provides an impetus for self-examination. It rattles our cages, shakes our paradigms, and sometimes blesses our enterprises. Being in service to a beloved cause is a joyful endeavor. We have chosen to be here, to do this.

And let's remember: the game is not about winning or losing. Defining it that way would perpetuate the Cult of Numbers madness that threatens to bring us down. James Carse, a professor of religion at New York University, reminds us that the point of the life game is to keep the ball in play.

We'll never have our act together. Once we give up that fantasy the show can go on. We can't beat the system by memorizing the rules. There are no rules—just myriad principles that reconfigure as they collide and mate, spontaneously giving birth to new principles even as we sleep.

We can work on mastering the anxiety we feel about inhabiting a reality that is penciled in. As Ilya Prigogine reminded us, it's an uncertain world in which perpetual change gives birth to new laws. If we can grasp this intellectually, our emotions and body knowledge will follow. We will recall a time when we sensed the opening of a doorway and stepped through.

The incidence of the miraculous seems to increase when we make an effort to do the right thing. It's as if a super-conscious intelligence thanks us for daring to transcend our habits.

Some projects seem to generate an uncommon number of paranormal events. People have described an accelerating field of frequencies surrounding certain enterprises. These apparent exceptions may be windows—dispensations rather than precedents, true at all times and in all places. Who knows? Maybe there are meta-principles uniquely and briefly arrayed for specific purposes.

As players learn to spin straw into gold and back again, we may learn something about the relative values of gold and straw. There will be no new game until we get the point of this one.

Our evolution as a species has been absurdly blessed with both a hospitable "nest" and the freedom to learn by making mistakes. We've been given keen radar for the good. Radical common sense enables us to perceive ourselves in space so that we can determine the ever-shifting radical center that is our real home.

The game is a metastory we're telling ourselves. Played well it reveals who and what we are, where we are going, and why we haven't arrived. We gradually see that we can't arrive at our destination by land or by sea but only by vision and pluck.

Serious playing is an addiction like no other. This is what we're made for: to work together in joyful service to God knows what. God knowing is enough.

• • •

Thoreau spoke of "that morrow which mere lapse of time can never make to dawn. The sun is but a morning star. Only that day dawns to which we are awake." Any day can be that morrow, the day that finds us awake. On any day we can concede that there is no certainty but calm in the face of all uncertainty; that simple next steps are suggested by our everyday wisdom.

We can wait for a thousand years, barring a calamity, or we can have it all now. Not by competing but by joining forces—as persons, as professions, as communities, as nations.

We ourselves are the "they" who would not let us do the right thing. "Their" traits are our own worst traits. Each of us can acknowledge our own hesitation, our closing down, our failure to speak up, our "waiting to see."

The hunger in the world is a reflection of our own nagging hunger for purpose; armies are an amplification of our warring selves; our depletion of Earth's resources reflects the depletion of our spirits.

The inner revolution is the heart of world revolution. The revolution underway is being launched by individuals everywhere declaring their freedom from self-repression. We ourselves are the problem and the solution. We can walk to freedom because it's never somewhere else. Imprisonment is a state of mind, not a condition of servitude.

Our myths and movies, our childlike sense of justice and play and magic, are not wrong. They are glimpses of a working-playing society yet to appear. Shall we stay in this, our present mind-set, a day longer than necessary, now that our liberators—our own brains and minds and cooperative spirits—have arrived?

Shall we linger to reminisce about the shared pain and injustice, or shall we leave now, taking only a few souvenirs to remind us of the price of habit?

There is a better place, the hard but joyful work beyond struggle, beyond the shadow of a doubt. It is our real home, the long-remembered future when everything worked and things made sense.

Pass the word.

APPENDIX

The Visionary Survey

More than two hundred "practicing visionaries," individuals who had successfully translated their visions more than once, filled out a detailed, six-page survey. They were asked to recall their earliest experience of carrying out a vision. They were queried about their parents, obstacles overcome, mistakes and lessons, and their ideas for educational reform.

One hundred were later asked to take a battery of tests normed on large populations, primarily in the workplace and educational settings. The testmakers expressed surprise at the pairing of traits that usually mutually exclusive.

On one test, the Birkman method, the respondents scored high in an index called "authority" (tends to take charge in a group) and yet extremely low in "advantage" (tends to look for personal advantage). In the workplace high scorers in "authority" usually score high in "authority."

High-energy subjects usually rebel against structure, but the visionary group tended to work well in organization.

On Ned Hermann's "Brain Dominance" profile, twenty-nine of the first thirty instruments sent in fell into the same quadrant—holistic, intuitive, integrative synthesizers. Hermann reported that the composite of the entire group was virtually identical to the composite of individuals recommended by the testmaker's network as "the most unusual person I know." According to Hermann the latter group "didn't think of themselves as unusual," just as our respondents hadn't thought of themselves as visionary.

On Anthony Gregorc's "Mind Styles" visionaries were typically "concrete random" thinkers as compared to abstract random, abstract sequential, or concrete sequential.

Parental encouragement was not especially predictive of visionary accomplishment. Many participants said they were driven to achieve "just to show" parents who had discouraged or actively opposed them.

For more information on the ongoing study, including the six-page questionnaire, write or visit the website. (See "Resources.")

RESOURCES

Arguelles, Jose. *The Transformative Vision*. Boston: Shambhala Publishing, 1975.

Augros, Robert and George Stanciu. *The New Story of Science*. Washington D.C.: Regnery Gateway, 1984.

Barber, Benjamin. *Strong Democracy*. Berkeley: University of California Press, 1984.

Brande, Dorothea. *Wake Up and Live!* New York: Simon & Schuster, 1980.

Briggs, John and David Peat. *Seven Life Lessons of Chaos*. New York: HarperCollins, 1999.

Briggs, John. *Fire in the Crucible*. Los Angeles: J.P. Tarcher, 1990.

Bruner, Jerome. *Beyond the Information Given*. New York: Norton, 1973.

Camus, Albert. "Create Dangerously." Lecture given at the University of Uppsala, Sweden, December 1957.

Carse, James. *Finite and Infinite Games: A Vision of Life as Play and Possibility*. New York: Ballantine, 1987.

Courtois, Flora, "The Door to Infinity." *Parabola*, 15 (2): Summer 1990.

Czikszentmihalyi, Mihali. *Flow: The Psychology of Optimal Experience*. New York: HarperCollins, 1990.

Daniels, Harry, ed. *Introduction to Vygotsky*. Oxford: Routledge, 1996.

De la Pena, Augustin. *The Psychobiology of Cancer*. Westport, CT: Praeger, 1983.

de Saint-Exupéry, Antoine. *Wind, Sand & Stars*. New York: Reynal & Hitchcock, 1939.

de Tocqueville, Alexis. *Democracy in America*. Paris: Gosselin, 1835.

Diamond, Marian. *Enriching Heredity*. New York: MacMillan, 1988.

Durrell, Lawrence. *The Spirit of Place*, ed. Alan Thomas. Berkeley: Marlowe & Company, 1997.

Eliot, T. S.. *Four Quartets*. New York: Harcourt, 1943.

Emerson, Ralph Waldo. *The Conduct of Life*. Boston: J.R. Osgood, 1871.

Fast, Howard. *The Hunter and the Trap*. New York: Dial Press, 1967.

Feldenkrais, Moshe. *The Potent Self*. New York: Harper & Row, 1985.

Ferrucci, Piero. *What We May Be*. Los Angeles: J. P. Tarcher, 1983.

Field, Joanna [Marian Milner]. *A Life of One's Own*. Los Angeles: J. P. Tarcher, 1981 [1936].

Gardner, Howard. *Frames of Mind: The Theory of Multiple Intelligence*. New York: Basic Books, 1981.

Gardner, Howard. *Multiple Intelligences After Twenty Years*. New York: Basic Books, 1993.

Gendlin, Eugene. *Focusing*. New York: Everest House, 1976.

Getzels, Jacob and Mihali Czikszentmihalyi. *The Creative Vision: A Longitudinal Study*. Hoboken: John Wiley & Sons, 1976.

Greider, William. *Who Will Tell the People?* New York: Simon & Schuster, 1992.

Hart, Leslie. *Human Brain and Human Learning*. Boston: Longman, 1984.

Heinlein, Robert. *Stranger in a Strange Land*. Boston: Houghton Mifflin, 1961.

Herrigel, Eugen. *Zen in the Art of Archery*. New York: Vintage Books, 1970.

Hofstadter, Douglas. *Metamagical Themas*. New York: Basic Books, 1985.

James, William. *The Principles of Psychology*. New York: Henry Holt, 1890.

Jung, C. G. *Synchronicity*. Princeton, NJ: Bollingen, 1973.

Kazantzakis, Nikos. *The Saviors of God*. New York: Simon & Schuster, 1960.

Kuhn, Thomas. *The Structure of Scientific Revolutions* (Third Ed.). Chicago: University of Chicago Press, 1996.

Leboyer, Frederic. *Birth Without Violence*. New York: Knopf, 1975.

Lemesurier, Peter. *Beyond All Belief*. New York: Lilian Barber Press, 1983.

MacLean, Paul. *The Triune Brain*. Columbus, OH: McGraw-Hill, 1976.

Maslow, Abraham. *The Farther Reaches of Human Nature*, New York: Viking, 1971.

Miller, Henry. *Wisdom of the Heart*. New York: New Directions, 1960.

Minsky, Marvin. *Society of Mind*. New York: Simon & Schuster, 1988.

Moffett, James. *The Universal Schoolhouse*. Hoboken: Jossey-Bass, 1994.

Montagu, Ashley. *Growing Young*. Columbus, OH: McGraw-Hill, 1989.

Montessori, Maria. *The Absorbent Mind*. New York: Henry Holt, 1967.

Moody, Raymond. *Life After Life*. New York: Bantam, 1975.

Peck, M. Scott. *The Road Less Traveled*. New York: Simon & Schuster, 1978.

Percy, Walker. *Lost in the Cosmos*. New York: Houghton Mifflin, 1983.

Prigogine, Ilya. *Order Out of Chaos*. New York: Bantam, 1984.

Rilke, Rainer Maria. *Selected Poems of Rainer Maria Rilke*, trans. Robert Bly. New York: Harper Perennial, 1981.

Ring, Kenneth. *Life At Death*. New York: Coward, McCann & Geoghegan, 1980.

Sheldrake, Rupert. *A New Science of Life*. New York: J. P. Tarcher, 1981.

Simonton, Dean Keith. *Greatness: Who Makes History and Why*. New York: The Guilford Press, 1994.

Smith, Page. *A New Age Now Begins: A People's History of the American Revolution*. New York: Penguin, 1989.

Snow, C. P. "Two Cultures," *The New Statesman*, 1956, and the Rede Lecture, 1959.

Sussman, Linda. *The Speech of the Grail*. Great Barrington, MA: Lindisfarne Books, 1995.

Thomas, Lewis. *The Lives of a Cell*. New York: Viking, 1974.

Wasserman, James. *The Slaves Shall Serve*. Athens, Greece: Sekmet Books, 2004.

Wills, Garry. *Lincoln at Gettysburg*. New York: Simon & Schuster, 1992.

Wilson, Colin. *The Outsider*. New York: Houghton Mifflin, 1956.

Wilson, Colin. *The Philosopher's Stone*. London: Granada, 1978.

Documentation for science cited in the book, links, periodicals, brain/mind summaries and other resources can be accessed at *www.aquariusnow.com* and *www.marilynferguson.com*.

INDEX

About the Author

MARILYN FERGUSON published *Brain/Mind Bulletin* from 1975 to 1995. Her work culled the best of the new consciousness movement and put the word out to seekers and movers and shakers on the grass-roots level. She offered commentary that has helped us launch a whole new way of looking at ourselves and the world we live in. She is the author of *The Brain Revolution* and *The Aquarian Conspiracy: Personal and Social Transformation in Our Time.*